The Librarians' Conference
of 1853

CHARLES B. NORTON

DANIEL C. GILMAN   S. HASTINGS GRANT

THE

Librarians' Conference of 1853

A CHAPTER IN AMERICAN LIBRARY HISTORY

BY

GEORGE BURWELL UTLEY

EDITED BY GILBERT H. DOANE

American Library Association

CHICAGO, 1951

Prefatory Note

As stated in the sketch of my uncle, this book was all but completed when he died. Even the final pages were in rough draft. As editor, I have finished it and have supplied most of the footnotes and the biographical references.

When Mr. Utley planned this book he did not anticipate the reproduction of the Proceedings of the Convention (see pages 129-176), hence Chapters Three to Seven, inclusive, may seem somewhat prolix. I have preferred to leave his résumé of the transactions as he wrote it rather than attempt a condensation, especially since no other alteration of his text has been made.

Undoubtedly Mr. Utley would have acknowledged his indebtedness to all who assisted him, but, unfortunately, the names of most of them were in his memory rather than recorded among his notes. He was especially grateful to Arthur Hastings Grant and Edith Grant, children of S. Hastings Grant, for their many courtesies and for the photograph which serves as frontispiece. Fragments of correspondence indicate that Mr. Utley received help from many librarians; as Editor, I, too, have had to depend upon the generosity of several more for data needed to identify some of the lesser known men who took part in the Conference of 1853. To all of these, unnamed as they so frequently are, I extend our gratitude.   G. H. D.

George Burwell Utley
1876-1946

GEORGE UTLEY REMARKED TO HIS WIFE ON THURSDAY EVENING, October 3rd, 1946, that he had practically finished his book. The next morning he went into his garden about nine thirty, as he usually did on fine days, to make it ready for the winter; for the Utleys expected to leave Pleasant Valley, their home in Connecticut, in about a fortnight to drive south to Winter Park where, for four years, they had spent the colder months. An hour or so later Mrs. Utley went out to speak to him and found him lying on the ground. He had had a fatal coronary thrombosis. Thus the earthly finis was written just as he was about to type the word at the end of this book, for undoubtedly he would have completed it that week.

Somehow, the quiet, unheralded manner of his death that sunny October day seemed a fitting close to his career. He died at the home of his youth and of his retirement, a place he had loved from earliest childhood, built by his maternal ancestors considerably more than a century and a half before, located in the quiet valley of the Farmington River, banked by the hills of western Connecticut. During his long years of professional life, Pleasant Valley, as the hamlet in the township of Barkhamstead is called, and Bur-well Heights, the old home place, had been his haven of rest each summer. He had delighted in keeping the house in repair and installing modern conveniences as they became feasible. There he and Mrs. Utley made their permanent home when he retired in 1942. There, surrounded by his books, without which life would have lost much of its flavor for him, he could look with ease on the wooded hills he loved. There he and his wife received, during the summer months, a constant stream of visitors, ranging from childhood friends and relatives to illustrious but none the less intimate friends of the professional and literary world, who often stopped to call or spend a night or two as they drove through the Litchfield Hills.

He began his life only twenty-five miles away in Hartford, where his father was in business. His mother died when he was a child and he was sent to the Valley, as he usually referred to it, to live with her sisters, the Misses Burwell. Thus, at an early age, Burwell Heights became truly his home. Later he was sent to Vermont Academy at Saxton's River, near Brattleboro. There he met Lou Gilbert, whom he married in 1901. From Vermont Academy he went to Colgate University, where he studied for a year only, and then transferred to Brown, where he earned the B. A. degree in 1899.

The teaching of English literature was his chosen field, but like many another young graduate, he did not find the job he was looking for immediately. While waiting for an appointment he went to work in the office of an insurance company in his native city and began to use the Watkinson Library. One day, a few weeks later, Mr. Frank B. Gay, the kindly librarian, a bookman of the old school, asked the young man if he would not be happier working with books than he was in the uncongenial atmosphere of a business office. Mr. Gay needed an assistant. "At least you'll be associated with books, if you work here!" So George Utley went to work in a library, much as did S. Hastings Grant and Daniel C. Gilman, two of the chief figures in the Conference of 1853. After an apprenticeship of two years, Utley was offered the librarianship of the Maryland Diocesan Library in Baltimore, then housed in the official residence of the Bishop of Maryland. On the third floor a small apartment was fitted up as a residence for the librarian. To this the young man brought his bride, the former schoolmate, Lou Gilbert, of Fairfield, Vermont, to set up housekeeping and begin their forty-five years of happy life together. And there George Utley first produced concrete evidence of his love of books, for he published a bibliographical essay on rare and unusual books in the Maryland Diocesan Library. This interest in rare and unusual books remained alive throughout his life, although during the period of his secretaryship of the American Library Association it was a personal interest only.

In 1905 the trustees of the Jacksonville Public Library offered him the librarianship, which he accepted, and the two New Englanders moved to a strange new world of alligators and oranges, live oaks and magnolias. They stayed there six years, during which he did much to improve and extend library service in Jacksonville. In 1911 the American Library Association was looking for a successor to Chalmers Hadley as its executive secretary. Mr. Utley, whose work in Florida had attracted attention, was chosen for the post, and the couple moved to Chicago, where the central office of the Association was located. Soon came the European War and the American Library Association's War Service program. Temporarily the Utleys moved to

Washington, where he plunged into the hectic work of supplying libraries and librarians for the training camps and
overseas centers, buying books and collecting them for
distribution to the service libraries. The late T. W. Koch,
one of Mr. Utley's closest associates in the work, told the
story in detail in his *Books in the War* (1919). Back in
Chicago after the armistice and the closing of the camp
libraries, the A.L.A. office had hardly readjusted to a peace-
time routine when in 1920 Mr. Edward L. Ryerson, President of the Board of Trustees of the Newberry Library,
called to see the Secretary and asked him if he would accept
the librarianship of that great library. Founded by a bequest of Walter Newberry, the library bearing his name
restricts its collections to belles lettres, history, music,
linguistics, and the book arts. Mr. W. N. C. Carleton's
resignation had been library news for some time, but it had
never entered George Utley's head that he might be thought
of as a successor to the post which William Frederick Poole,
one of the men of whom he writes in this book, had initiated
with great distinction and for which he had set a high
standard of achievement. In view of his own training in
English literature, his love for books as physical objects as
well as for their contents, he quite naturally was much attracted to the opportunity which the administration of a
library such as the Newberry presented, and he accepted
the post.

For the next twenty-two and a half years he was its chief
librarian, taking a great personal interest in the acquisition
of treasure after treasure: a block book and hundreds of
incunabula for the Wing Foundation, rarities in English
literature, source material in American history. He enjoyed
greatly contacts with scholars and other men of letters—

books in the making—as they came to the Newberry to use its collections and to his office for consultation in bibliographical problems. His advice was freely given; his balanced judgment, his knowledge of literature and history, of books and of libraries containing them, making it of inestimable value to an untold number of patrons. In his relationships with his staff his great humanity made itself most evident. His office was always open to any fellow worker who needed advice, who wanted to talk over a problem, even if it was a personal one, for George Utley learned early in his administrative experience that personal problems have a bearing on the efficiency of any staff worker. His sympathy went out to those who worked with him and his candor and tact made it easy for them to talk with him.

In 1941, the Board of Trustees of the Newberry Library decided to adopt a retirement policy patterned after that prevailing in many universities. Thus sixty-five became the retirement age for the staff. George Utley was then in his sixty-fifth year, so it was arranged that he would become librarian emeritus the first of September, 1942. Even though it was not easy for him to relinquish his hope of finishing out a quarter of a century as Newberry's librarian, he accepted retirement philosophically and Pleasant Valley became once more his permanent home. For four years, one month and four days as a man of leisure, he found much to do; and he did it with his usual quiet calm, enjoying to the full his garden and his car, his books and his friends, his work on this book, and the opportunity to travel as leisurely as he wished, for he was one of those who really enjoyed travel (the unpublished journal of the Utleys' three week motor trip from Winter Park to Pleasant Valley in 1946 is a joy to read).

While at the Maryland Diocesan Library, he began his first book, *The Life and Times of Thomas John Claggett, First Bishop of Maryland* (Chicago, 1913). Shortly after he became Secretary of the American Library Association he became interested in the Librarians' Conference of 1853, the first meeting of librarians as a professional group. Through contact with Arthur Hastings Grant, son of Seth Hastings Grant, the secretary of that conference, the A.L.A. came into possession of Grant's papers, the correspondence relative to and the records of that initial convention. Finding little in print about the Conference and all of that buried in journals and newspapers, he began work on this book. Before he completed it William Murray's reprint of the proceedings, published by The Torch Press in Cedar Rapids, was published, but that did not deter him, for Mr. Murray merely reprinted, without comment or background, the transactions as given in *Norton's Literary and Educational Register, for 1854*. However, the declaration of war against Germany in 1917 and the A.L.A.'s decision to set up its War Service program did make it necessary for him to lay aside his work, which he did not find time to resume until after his retirement in 1942. He had completed all but a dozen pages of the final draft when death intervened.

Meanwhile, during his professional career he wrote a good deal for library magazines, and prepared many papers and addresses, not a few of which found their way into print. In 1926, at the time of the semicentennial of the A.L.A., he read a paper before the Chicago Literary Club which he called *Fifty Years of the American Library Association*. This the Association, which he had served as president in 1922-3, published as its official recognition of its anniversary. His annual reports as librarian of the Newberry, more or less couched in official language (his love of words and feeling for style could never be entirely disguised even in reports), are bibliographically interesting. Reading between their lines one can discern much of the man who wrote them.

George Utley's attitude toward his profession, the profession which chose him rather than that of his choice, inspired many a young person to librarianship. His honesty, his candor, his tact, his sympathy, his humanity, his knowledge and love of books, his grace and ease in social gatherings, his interest in people, his ability to talk about books and affairs, as well as his enjoyment in listening to others talk, rendered him a notable figure in the world in which he moved.

GILBERT H. DOANE

Table of Contents

Chapter One

"We meet to provide for the diffusion of a knowledge of good books and for enlarging the means of public access to them. Our wishes are for the public, not for ourselves."

These words, as appropriate at a gathering of librarians today as they were nearly one hundred years ago, were spoken by Charles Coffin Jewett, on Thursday morning, September 15, 1853. Jewett, who held the post of Librarian of the recently established Smithsonian Institution, had just been chosen president of the first Convention of Librarians to be held in this country, and, so far as known, the first to be held in the world.

In response to a call which had been sent out earlier in the year eighty-two men had gathered that September morning in what was known as the Smaller Chapel of New York University, down in Washington Square. The room in which they met was austere in its furnishings. Plain wooden benches, looking much like the pews one finds in meeting-houses of the mid-nineteenth century, ran in semicircles around a low platform on which stood an unembellished pulpit, bearing tall glass-enclosed gas lights at either end. A row of straight-backed, uncomfortable-looking chairs was lined up in uncompromising stiffness behind the rostrum. The walls were unadorned: innocent of pictures, frescoes, or decorations of any kind. Thus the Chapel, where the undergraduates were compelled to attend service every morning, looked in 1853, and so it continued to look until 1894 when the building of which it was a part was demolished soon after the University removed to its present uptown location at University Heights.

All the delegates were men. The day of women in library work had not arrived, in fact it had not arrived to any considerable extent in commercial fields. A woman in business was so rare that to learn of one was news, as evidenced by this item in the *New York Observer* of September 15, 1853, the very day the librarians were meeting:

"At one of the largest wholesale warehouses in Boston the head corresponding clerk is a young woman, who writes a beautiful rapid hand, and fulfills the duties of the situation to the complete satisfaction of her liberal employer."

While the librarians were placidly conferring in the Smaller Chapel of New York University other important events were taking place in the world at large.

Commodore Perry was forcing the Japanese to open their ports to the trade of the world, an event the full significance and consequences of which would not be realized until many years later.

Franklin Pierce, in the preceding March, had begun a rather uneventful four-years' reign in the White House at Washington.

In France, Louis Napoleon had, within the year, become Emperor of the French and that January had married Eugenie, the daughter of a Spanish grandee.

Over the Alps in Italy Count Cavour had, in the previous November, become premier and in the succeeding seven years would play an important rôle in the political life of Europe. And in the following March the soldiers of England and Russia would be plunged into the Crimean War. And nearer home, rail connections were established in 1853 between New York and Chicago.

The librarians were, we hope, well-informed citizens of the world and cognizant of these affairs, but no hints of them appear in the proceedings of the Convention, so far as they have been preserved.

The eighty-two members comprising this historic gathering had registered their names, addresses, and positions at the near-by bookstore of Charles B. Norton, 71 Chambers Street, and the secretary had called the roll, asking each delegate to rise and be identified as his name was reached[1].

From that Thursday morning, September 15, until Saturday noon, the 17th, these men ground out an astonishingly large grist of library and bibliographic business. They made speeches, some prepared, others apparently extemporaneous, on various aspects of their common interests, read papers on cataloging, classifying and indexing, on exchanges between libraries, on the proper selection of books, on better distribution of government documents, and adopted over a score of resolutions. Although few of these resolutions were carried out they, and the deliberations which led to them, had an important even though indirect influence on libraries and librarians for many years. This first convention began a new era in American librarianship and the effects and impetus had not been entirely dissipated when librarians met in Philadelphia in 1876, nearly a quarter century later, and formed the permanent organization, the American Library Association. But the influence exerted by the 1853 meeting was so indirect that succeeding generations of librarians have been more or less unaware and unconscious of it. References to it are to be found scattered through the library literature of the thirty or forty years following the event, but over the past fifty years mention of it has been rare; and doubtless many of the forty-odd thousand men and women now engaged in library work know little or nothing about that first gathering of their craft on those September days in 1853.

Five men initiated and worked out the arrangements for the Convention and it seems not difficult to determine with reasonable accuracy the share of each. These men were: Charles Coffin Jewett, librarian of the Smithsonian Institution; Charles Benjamin Norton, bookseller and publisher of New York; Seth Hastings Grant, librarian of the New York Mercantile Library; Reuben Aldridge Guild, librarian of Brown University; and Daniel Coit Gilman, a recent graduate of Yale, from whom the educational world was later to hear.

Of the last two I have personal recollections. As an undergraduate at Brown in the late nineties I went one evening to hear Dr. Guild, by that time the venerable librarian-emeritus, give a talk on early days in the Brown University Library. And in 1902, in Baltimore, where I was then engaged in library work, I was so fortunate as to be present at the impressive ceremonies attending the twenty-fifth anniversary of Johns Hopkins University and the twenty-fifth anniversary likewise of its distinguished president, Daniel C. Gilman, who, with tact and dignity, presided over that two-day celebration. At one of the sessions a letter of affection and congratulation, signed by over a thousand Hopkins graduates, was presented to President Gilman.[2] The Hopkins man chosen to make the presentation was Woodrow Wilson, then professor of jurisprudence at Princeton.

But we digress, and will get back to the time when Dan

Gilman was twenty-two and had just graduated from Yale. Over thirty years after the Convention Dr. Guild wrote: "Professor Jewett was to my certain knowledge the prime mover, although Charles B. Norton first proposed it in the columns of his *Gazette*."[3] William F. Poole, first librarian of the Newberry Library, said in his presidential address at the American Library Association conference of 1886, that Jewett was "the ablest and most zealous of the early American reformers in the methods of library administration" and was "the leading spirit in the call and management of the [1853] Convention."[4] Guild was unquestionably right in calling Jewett the "prime mover," in the sense that he was the most *prominent* mover, for he was the leading figure in the American library field of that day, and the one who would certainly be consulted regarding plans under way, because his approval of measures was desired and sought and much weight was given to his opinion. And Guild was probably also right in stating that the proposal first came from Charles B. Norton.

Jewett was a graduate of Brown University in the class of 1835 and served as its librarian and professor of modern languages for a number of years prior to his appointment, in 1848, as assistant secretary and librarian of the recently founded Smithsonian Institution. His tenure of office, however, lasted for only six years, for he and Joseph Henry, secretary of the Institution, came to such absolute disagreement that Jewett was compelled to resign. Henry wanted all the income from James Smithson's bequest used for the preparation and publication of scientific works for the promotion and diffusion of knowledge. Jewett wanted half of the income to be devoted to the upbuilding of a national library at the Smithsonian. Although the Congress ap-

5

proved Jewett's plan and so voted, Henry had his way and the librarian's ambitious designs for a great library were sidetracked and he was, as we have said, forced to resign.

The perspective of time has shown that things have worked out for the best. The incalculable service which the Smithsonian Institution has rendered to science through its research projects and its publication would have been far less if half its income had been diverted over all these years to the purchase of books and the administration of them; and the Library of Congress has become, in the last fifty years, our national library to an extent far surpassing the rosiest dreams which Charles Jewett could possibly have had.

The newly organized Boston Public Library was quick to acquire Jewett and, as soon as there was a vacancy, made him superintendent, as its head was then called. He held that honorable and prominent post until his sudden death, by apoplexy, in 1868. His magnetic personality and influence were felt for years. During the first quarter century of the American Library Association scarcely an annual conference passed at which his name was not mentioned with appreciation of his services. His *Notices of Public Libraries in the United States of America,* published by the Smithsonian Institution in 1851, was the first extended collection of facts and figures on American libraries. At the time of the 1853 Convention Jewett was thirty-seven years old.

Charles B. Norton was an editor and publisher and an agent for American libraries. He was in the book business in Boston previous to 1848. Then he removed to New York and was with D. Appleton & Company a couple of years when he went into business for himself. He specialized in helping college, mercantile and other libraries build up their book collections. In those days when a voyage to

6

Europe was an event in any man's life he made frequent trips to England and the European continent, buying for his American clients. By 1853 he was conducting what was then a large book and periodical importing business. It was he who in 1853, a few weeks before the Convention, published the first trade edition of Poole's *Index to Periodical Literature.* Norton traveled about this country in the interest of his business and on such trips saw and talked with many librarians. It is easy to believe that it was he, with his keen business sagacity, who first thought of the idea and suggested that librarians get together and talk over matters of mutual concern. Such a meeting would certainly be grist to his mill. He was energetic, resourceful, and seems to have had real solicitude for the development of libraries quite independent of his commercial interests. He was editor and publisher of *Norton's Literary Gazette,* a monthly, and *Norton's Literary and Educational Register,* an annual. A decade later he was prominent in the Civil War, attaining the rank of brigadier general. After that conflict he did not return to the publishing field but became actively concerned with the business end of fairs and expositions and had a hand in the Paris Exposition of 1867 and in the Centennial Exhibition of 1876. He died in Chicago, at the Palmer House, in January, 1891, having gone there a few days previously in connection with some business of the Columbian Exposition, plans for which were getting under way. He was born in Hartford, Connecticut, in 1825, and, notwithstanding his prominent place in the book world, was only twenty-eight years old at the time of the Convention.

With his time fully occupied by other matters Norton left the editing of the *Gazette,* and the *Register* too, for that matter, in the capable hands of two assistant editors, Seth Hastings Grant and Daniel Coit Gilman. Both of these young men held other positions and their editorial duties were distinctly secondary.

Seth Hastings Grant was, as we have said, librarian of the New York Mercantile Library, which corresponded more to a modern public circulating library of popular literature than any other institution in the city. He was an intelligent and able young man and well thought of by all who knew him.[5] After serving in that position for seventeen years, from 1849 to 1866, he resigned and went into business, doubtless feeling the necessity of something more lucrative to meet the needs of a growing family. He was a broker and realtor for six years, superintendent of the New York Produce Exchange for five more, comptroller of the City of New York for two years, and ended his business career as vice-president of the United States National Bank. In his later years he was active in historical society circles, compiled a book on New York City in the Revolutionary War,[6] and was an elder in the Presbyterian Church. He lived to a good old age, passing away when in his eighties, as recently as the year 1910. Grant was secretary of the 1853 Convention and in 1915 his son, Arthur Hastings Grant, of Elizabeth, New Jersey, gave to the American Library Association his father's papers, documents, and correspondence relating to that gathering, and this unpublished material has been drawn upon in the preparation of this monograph. At the time of the Convention Grant was only twenty-five years old.

Daniel Coit Gilman, the future president of Johns Hopkins University, was the youngest member of the group, being only twenty-two at that time. He had graduated from Yale the year before, 1852, and had gone down to New York from his home in Norwich, Connecticut, where his father had made a comfortable fortune manufacturing nails, to help catalog the Mercantile Library under the supervision of Hastings Grant, whom he spoke of in a family letter as his dearest friend outside his own kin. From their intimacy grew their joint editorship of *Norton's Literary Gazette,* an excellent and highly creditable periodical, which came nearer being a library journal than any other magazine published in this country before the advent of the *Library Journal,* which began publication in 1876.

Three months after the Convention Gilman and his life-long friend, Andrew Dickson White, who had that year graduated from Yale, went to Europe and spent the next two years as attachés of the United States legation at St. Petersburg. Both returned to this country in 1855, White going to the University of Michigan to teach for a few years before entering on his great work of founding Cornell, and Gilman going back to Yale, where for seventeen years he was librarian and professor of geography. Then he was president of the recently established University of California for three years, but state legislative measures hampered him and he welcomed the call to organize a new research university in Baltimore which had just been made possible through the bequest of the railroad financier, Johns Hopkins. It is pleasant for librarians to recall that this distinguished scholar, Daniel C. Gilman, was, "from his youth up," actively concerned with library affairs.

The fifth member of this group responsible for bringing the Librarians' Convention into being was Reuben Aldridge Guild, who was at that time thirty-one years old. A graduate of Brown University, he had been librarian of his Alma Mater for five years, succeeding his former teacher, Charles

9

Jewett, when the latter resigned to go to the Smithsonian. Devoted to Brown, Guild became an authority on its history and on the history of the little state of which it is the chief institution of higher education. When he retired in 1893, William Frederick Poole became the sole surviving member of the 1853 Convention remaining in active library work, and he passed away in March of the following year.

These, then, are the five men responsible for bringing about the world's first convention of librarians, and their respective shares of participation appear to be something like this: The idea of a convention probably first came from the active business brain of Norton who passed it on to his assistants, Grant and Gilman, to be thought about and fanned into life; that, as was their custom, the three discussed the matter with their close associate, Reuben Guild, a frequent contributor to the *Gazette;* and that then they approached and conferred with Jewett, recognizing him as America's leading librarian, whose co-operation must be secured if the gathering was to be a success. Then the wheels were set in motion by an editorial in *Norton's Literary Gazette,* perhaps written by Norton himself, but more likely by either Grant or Gilman.

This editorial, the first suggestion on the subject in print, so far as we can discover, appeared in the *Gazette* of July 15, 1852,[7] fourteen months before the Convention was held. It began by stating that the idea of having a convention of librarians and others interested in bibliographical studies had been discussed "to some extent for a considerable time past." The American Association for the Advancement of Science, at that time four years old, was expecting to meet in Cleveland in August of that year, and it was suggested that perhaps that time and place would be as convenient as any for the meeting of the librarians. The proper way to accomplish the desired object, it was felt, would be to have some of the librarians of the larger institutions unite in calling such a meeting. Their names would be a guarantee for the interest in the gathering and "would insure a large assembly." The topics for discussion, the editorial went on to say, would be almost "innumerable." Aside from papers on bibliographical subjects, there were a great many points in regard to the management of libraries, the purchase and arrangement of books, the formation and publication of catalogs, the delivery of books, their protection from mold, worms, and other injury, on almost all of which points there existed, it was said, a difference of opinion, or, at any rate, of practice. Indeed, said the writer, we have hardly ever known two librarians to agree upon these minor matters, so that a little discussion could not fail to elicit various observations and suggestions by which all might be benefited.

True to editorial form the article was unsigned and we do not positively know who first rang the bell. But, as we have said, it is our opinion that the editorial came from the pen of either Hastings Grant or Daniel Gilman.

Nothing tangible resulted from this feeler. For one thing the Science Association did not hold its expected meeting that year. Even had it done so the time between July 15 and some time in August would have been too short to work up a successful conference. But the leaven had apparently begun to work, for some interest was shown and response made, it was stated, in a brief editorial in the *Gazette,* two months later, September 15, 1852.[8]

Nothing further on the subject is found in that periodical until February 15, 1853,[9] when an editorial of some seven hundred words appeared. Its theme was encouragement of a proposal to hold a convention some time during the coming summer at the time and place of the Science Association meeting. The editorial then went on to give reasons again why such a convention was needed and why there was good prospect for its success.

Hundreds of libraries more or less public, Mercantile, Mechanic, Social, Collegiate and State, are already in vigorous operation, new enterprises are constantly started, and as one after another of our Western cities spring up to rival its Eastern predecessors, the Library is regularly to hold no unimportant place among the public undertakings. The importance of having these various institutions well managed, demands more careful consideration than it usually receives. Anyone who, in traveling from city to city, has visited the Libraries, will be struck with the differences which they exhibit where external conditions appear to be nearly the same— the size of the town and the intelligence of the inhabitants. It is the management, he will see, which makes the difference. If he is accustomed to the elegance of the Boston Athenaeum, the enterprise of the New York Mercantile, the limited but skilful arrangements at Williams College, the scholar-like commencement of the Smithsonian Library, and the convenience of other well-ordered libraries, he will be surprised at the contrast which is often presented where the funds are as great, but where the same judgment has not been displayed in their control.

So the writer went on to make his purport clear: let us get together, compare experiences, and see if greater efficiency will not result from an exchange of views.

Whatever may have been Hastings Grant's part in the earlier editorials I doubt if he wrote this one, because, judging from his general character as we know it, he was too modest to refer to "the enterprise of the New York Mercantile," of which he was the head. Our surmise is that it was penned by Norton himself. When the writer refers to "anyone who, in traveling from city to city, has visited the Libraries," it looks like a reference to Norton's own experiences, for that was just what he was doing a good deal of his time.

The March number of the *Gazette* bore the first suggestion that the Convention be held in New York.

We continue to receive assurances from various quarters of the land, of the interest which is felt in this enterprise. It has been suggested by some that the desire which will be generally felt this summer for visiting the Great Exhibition, and the low rates of travel to this city, will make New York the most fitting place for this meeting.[10]

New York truly seemed in most respects the logical place, much more so a hundred years ago than Cleveland, and doubtless would have been chosen even had there been no special magnet, such as the great industrial exhibition held that year in the Crystal Palace, erected on the block just west of where the New York Public Library now stands at Fifth Avenue and Forty-second Street. It imitated, as much as it could, the Great Crystal Palace Exhibition of 1851, in London, the enterprise so enthusiastically espoused by Prince Albert, Queen Victoria's consort. President Franklin Pierce came up from Washington to attend the opening of the New York fair on July 14.

This meeting of 1853 held at the time and place of an exposition set a precedent which has been followed by librarians on numerous subsequent occasions. The American Library Association came into being at the Philadelphia Centennial in 1876, and the Association met conjointly with the Columbian Exposition in Chicago in 1893, the Louisiana Purchase Exposition at St. Louis in 1904, the Lewis and Clark in Portland in 1905, at Berkeley in 1915 in close proximity to the Panama-Pacific International Exposition across the Bay, at Chicago again in 1933, the year of A Century of Progress, and at San Francisco in 1939 when the beautiful fair was in full swing on Treasure Island.

The April issue of *Norton's Literary Gazette* reported that the desire for a Librarians' Convention was spreading.

Among other things pertaining thereto which have reached us since our last, is a letter from a prominent librarian of Philadelphia, urging New York for the place, instead of Cleveland, and recommending the month of October for the time. That month, however, is, we think, more likely to be a busy time with College Librarians than September. Letters from Cincinnati and St. Louis assure us of the co-operation of librarians at the West. We hope to receive still more of such letters from other librarians, both far and near.[11]

The May number of the *Gazette*[12] announced that at length success for the project seemed assured, that a formal Call, signed by prominent librarians in various cities, was about to be sent forth, naming New York as the place and September as the time. The proposal to meet in Cleveland in conjunction with the seventh conference of the American Association for the Advancement of Science did not prove popular.

"Cleveland is too far away," wrote A. J. Upson,[13] librarian and professor of rhetoric in Hamilton College, "and it seems as if the subject will be of sufficient importance and interest to bring men together. I hope the Convention will be called at New York in the early part of September."

"I take considerable interest," wrote J. Berrien Lindsley,[14] of Nashville, to Norton on June 19, "in the proposed Librarians' Convention. With you I think New York is the place, and by all means September the time, say about the 10th or 15th." Although the time and place met Lindsley's suggestions, neither he nor any other delegate from Tennessee was present at the Convention.

Charles E. West,[15] of Buffalo, wrote: "I like the idea of a Librarians' Convention. Would be most happy to attend if it could be appointed in August or later than the 15th of September. Our term will open about that time which will confine me here." Then as now it seemed impossible to fix the date for a conference convenient to everybody.

Chapter Two

WITH THE PLACE AND DATE SETTLED, THE FOLLOWING CALL for the Convention was drafted, probably by Norton or Grant, possibly by Jewett, and printed in the *Gazette* of May 15, 1853:[16]

CALL

The undersigned, believing that the knowledge of books, and the foundation and management of collections of them for public use, may be promoted by consultation and concert among librarians and others interested in bibliography, respectfully invite such persons to meet IN CONVENTION AT NEW YORK, ON THURSDAY, THE FIFTEENTH DAY OF SEPTEMBER, for the purpose of conferring together upon the means of advancing the prosperity and usefulness of public libraries, and for the suggestion and discussion of topics of importance to book collectors and readers.

MAY, 1853.

CHAS. FOLSOM, *Boston Athenaeum.*

C. C. JEWETT, *Smithsonian Institution.*

T. W. HARRIS, *Harvard College.*

PHILIP J. FORBES, *Society Library, New York.*

SAMUEL F. HAVEN, *American Antiquarian Society.*

BARNAS SEARS, *Massachusetts State Library.*

E. C. HERRICK, *Yale College.*

JOSHUA LEAVITT, *American Geographical and Statistical Society.*

EDWARD E. HALE, *Worcester, Mass.*
HENRY BARNARD, *Hartford, Ct.*
J. W. CHAMBERS, *American Institute.*
WM. E. JILLSON, *Providence, R. I.*
A. J. UPSON, *Hamilton College.*
JAMES GREEN, *Baltimore Mercantile Library.*
W. A. JONES, *Columbia College.*
R. A. GUILD, *Brown University.*
G. H. MOORE, *New York Historical Society.*
W. F. POOLE, *Boston Mercantile Library.*
N. B. SHURTLEFF, *American Academy of Arts and Sciences.*
S. HASTINGS GRANT, *New York Mercantile Library.*
L. M. BOLTWOOD, *Amherst College.*
WM. P. CURTIS, *St. Louis Mercantile Library.*
R. H. STEPHENSON, *Cincinnati Mercantile Library.*
H. M. BAILEY, *Hartford Young Men's Institute.*
GEO. E. DAY, *Lane Seminary.*
LLOYD P. SMITH, *Philadelphia Library Company.*

This is the list of signers as printed on a leaflet copy of
the Call, dated September 5, 1853, and in the Proceedings
of the Convention in *Norton's Literary and Educational
Register, for 1854* (p. 49-50). The list as printed in the
Gazette of May 15, 1853 is the same except that it lacks the
names of Henry Barnard, James Green, William F. Poole,
L. M. Boltwood, and H. M. Bailey and includes the name
of the Rev. E. H. Chapin, of New York.[17] The omission of
Chapin's name from the final draft was probably an error,
and not because he objected to having it included, inasmuch
as he was present at the Convention.

We do not know the procedure used to obtain signatures.
The original copy may have been signed by librarians and
others who happened to visit Norton's bookshop and it may
have been taken along by Norton on business trips to nearby

cities. We know that in the early summer Gilman visited Boston and Cambridge and perhaps he stopped at New Haven and Providence on the way. He *may* have returned by way of Worcester and Hartford and he *may* have carried a copy of the Call with him and so obtained the names of the signers in those cities. But all this, we confess, is conjecture. We have no proof to support it. Jewett, in his opening address as president, said,

The Call for this Convention was not the result of a correspondence among librarians, nor was it the subject of long and careful consideration. It was, rather, a spontaneous movement. It was first, I think, suggested a year ago, or more, in the *Literary Gazette*. Librarians spoke to each other on the matter, when they happened to meet. Everyone was pleased with the idea. At length a formal call was written, and signed by a few who happened to meet the gentlemen having charge of the paper.[18]

We cannot, however, believe that the gathering of names was quite so casual and indiscriminate as that, for the Call included the names, rather carefully arranged as to prominence, of nearly all the leading librarians of the period, together with those of a few gentlemen who represented important societies or organizations and whose interest in library development or bibliographical studies would lend weight or influence.

First on the list was the fifty-nine year old Charles Folsom, acknowledged *Nestor* of his craft, graduate of Harvard and for a time its librarian, distinguished both for his personal accomplishments and for the post he then held as head of the highly respected Boston Athenaeum.

Comment has already been made on Charles C. Jewett, the second signer, and on S. Hastings Grant, whose name appears seventh from the end. The names of Charles B.

Norton and Daniel C. Gilman do not appear, Norton's possibly because he considered that the name of a bookseller and publisher would not be appropriate. Perhaps Gilman did not sign because of his youth and the subordinate position he held in library circles.

Among the others who signed that historic document are these:

Thaddeus W. Harris, better remembered, it must be confessed, as an entomologist than for bibliothecal accomplishments, was, like his father before him, librarian of Harvard, a post he had held for twenty-five years.[19]

Edward C. Herrick had been for the preceding ten years librarian of Yale, and although his eminence as an economic entomologist and astronomer (a curious mating of specialties!) outshone his reputation as a librarian, his official position gave weight to his name on the document.[20]

George H. Moore, New Hampshire born and a graduate of the University of New York, was actively connected with the New York Historical Society, either as assistant librarian, librarian, or member of its executive committee for over fifty years—from 1841 until his death in 1892. For the last twenty years of his life he was superintendent and trustee of the Lenox Library, that storehouse of rare Americana, founded by his friend, the austere James Lenox. Possessing the flair for historical study conspicuous in his father, Jacob Bailey Moore, and his brother, the voluminous writer, Frank Moore, he was a patient and careful investigator in the colonial and revolutionary periods of American history and assembled an important personal library, the sale of which in 1893 was one of the notable book auctions of that day.[21]

William Alfred Jones, then in his middle thirties, friend

of many of the literary luminaries of the period, had been librarian of Columbia College for two years and was bringing its library rapidly into a position of usefulness and influence.[22]

Barnas Sears, who two years later would assume the presidency of Brown University and be a vital force in higher education, was librarian of the Massachusetts State Library and secretary of the Massachusetts Board of Education, succeeding Horace Mann in this position.[23]

Lloyd Pearsall Smith was one of the best known librarians of his day. Succeeding his father in 1851 as head of the ancient and honorable Library Company of Philadelphia, founded by Benjamin Franklin and his friends, he was identified with it until his death in 1886. He was one of the few "conventioners" of 1853 who lived to take an active part in the work of the American Library Association.[24]

William Frederick Poole, thirty-two years old, graduate of Yale in the class of '49 (his failure to graduate until he was twenty-eight years old caused by lack of money), was destined to become the most distinguished librarian who signed the Call and attended the Convention. At that time he was librarian of the Boston Mercantile Library, but later in his long and notable career he was the chief executive of the public libraries of Cincinnati and Chicago, and left the latter post in 1887 to become the first librarian of the new institution founded on the bequest of Walter Loomis Newberry. So far as the proceedings show Poole took no part in the three-day discussions, which fact is hard to reconcile with his later ever-readiness to plunge into debate and controversy.[25]

Of the nonlibrarians who signed the Call and attended the Convention the one to become the most widely known was Edward Everett Hale. He was then thirty-one years old and minister of the Church of the Unity in Worcester. He had not yet acquired that wide reputation as preacher and writer that we now think of as his. Ten years later the *Atlantic Monthly*[26] would print his "The Man Without a Country," generally acknowledged to be one of the best short stories to come from the pen of an American; but even by 1853 Hale was already many-sided in his interests and looked on the growth of mechanic and mercantile libraries with sympathy and approbation.[27]

Gratefully remembered also by his fellow Americans is that zealous educator, Henry Barnard, who shares with Horace Mann the honor of being a pioneer of the free school system of America. Barnard graduated from Yale in 1830, later held college presidencies and in 1867 became the first United States Commissioner of Education. By 1853 he was already well launched on his distinguished educational career and at that time, as superintendent of schools of his native state of Connecticut, was apparently able to envision what more and better libraries would mean in connection with more and better schools.[28]

Not all of the twenty-six who signed the Call attended the Convention. Harris of Harvard and Herrick of Yale were prevented by college duties and sent apologies and regrets. Nathanael B. Shurtleff, who signed as representative of the American Academy of Arts and Sciences, was well known as a writer in his day, was thrice mayor of Boston (1868-70) and a trustee of its public library.[29] Joshua Leavitt was active in journalistic enterprises and assistant editor of the *Independent* and a trustee of the American Geographical and Statistical Society.[30] These men probably had no expectation of attending when they signed but lent their names in the "interest of a good cause" very much as public-spirited citizens of later generations have done. There was clearly an effort to have all sections of the country represented, for among the signers were James Green, of Baltimore, R. H. Stephenson, of Cincinnati, and W. P. Curtis, of St. Louis. They were the librarians of the mercantile libraries in their respective home cities and all three were present to answer to the roll-call.[31]

All in all, it was a notable and distinguished list of names. If inclusion in the *Dictionary of American Biography* can be accepted as a criterion to indicate fame, or, at least, distinction, it may be worth noting that fourteen, one more than half who signed this document calling together the world's first congress of librarians, are included in that compendium. But that is not the whole picture, for sixteen other members of the Convention who were not signers of the Call were deemed by the editors of the *Dictionary* important enough to have their careers recorded in its pages. In other words, of the 82 delegates, 30, or over a third, are "in" the D.A.B.[32]

Every eastern state from Maine to Maryland was represented at the Convention, except New Hampshire, Vermont and Delaware, and, in addition, there were delegates from Cincinnati, Columbus, St. Louis, New Orleans and San Francisco. It is hard to believe that the man who registered from San Francisco came all the way expressly to attend that meeting. In 1853 one could not run out and jump aboard an overland limited and alight in Chicago two days later, not to mention the air miracle of breakfast in San Francisco and dinner in New York. Then, at best it was the Isthmus of Panama; at worst Cape Horn. We think he must have combined attendance with other transcontinental errands.

But, however it may be, there he is, "Edward E. Dunbar, Mercantile Library, San Francisco." Only four years after the great California gold rush of '49! He was a trustee of the institution he represented, but shortly after 1853 he severed his connection with it and left California. He was undoubtedly in New York on business.[33]

Except for two men from New Orleans there were no representatives from the great block of states which, a decade later, constituted the Confederate States of America. Perhaps young men's mercantile and mechanics libraries found poor soil where labor was based on the institution of slavery.

The name of one prominent librarian, that of the eccentric sixty-seven-year-old Joseph Green Cogswell,[34] was missing, not only from the Call but also from the list of Convention delegates. Cogswell was abroad, buying books for the soon-to-be-opened Astor Library when the Call was being circulated, and when the 15th of September came around he was spending all his energy and time putting the finishing touches on the new building and collection of reference books provided by the bequest of John Jacob Astor. Though Cogswell was too busy, or thought he was, to look in at the Smaller Chapel of the University and become a part of this chapter of library history there being enacted he showed his interest and good wishes in an apology for absence which he sent over and which was read on the first day. He arranged also to have the delegates attend in a body a reception at the Astor Library after they adjourned on Friday afternoon, their second day, and before they attended a reception that evening at the Kemble House, around on 19th Street, tendered them by their New York colleagues.

News of the proposed Convention duly reached England and elicited comment from at least a few English librarians and from certain literary journals. The London *Critic* had this to say:

A certain *esprit de corps* and desire for organization and mutual improvement seems to be growing up among the Librarians of the United States, and to promise results which we in England may find it worth our while to cultivate. Last summer a suggestion was thrown out in the States for the holding of a "Convention of Librarians," immediately after the meeting of the Scientific Association at Clevelend; and it would appear that the suggestion is likely this year to assume a practical shape, and meet with the realization which was denied it last. . . . We wish the movement all success, and would cordially desire that a similar one for a Convention of the Secretaries of Literary Institutes were already inaugurated at home.[35]

Kitto's Journal of Sacred Literature also recognized the movement:

It has been proposed in New York that a convention of librarians should be held at some convenient time and place for consultation about various matters pertaining to "the craft." By such a convention the experience of long-established institutions, and their well-trained conductors, might be so brought out as to inform and benefit the more recent establishments and the less accomplished librarians. Such a convention would be useful among us who have so many institutions and printing societies. . . .[36]

Norton went to Europe early that summer to purchase books for various American libraries and described a call he made on the dynamic head of the British Museum, Sir Anthony Panizzi. To his assistant editor, S. Hastings Grant, he wrote from London on July 12, 1853:

. . . The last number of the *Gazette* pleases me much especially about the Convention. All the Librarians here are talking about it. I have been at the Museum for the last four hours and have had a regular chat with Panizzi and Watts.[37] The *Gazette* had but just come in and Panizzi was looking it over. They both expressed great pleasure at the matters to be talked about and came to the conclusion that it would take at least a month . . . "Vell," Panizzi says, "you young men in America are certainly very quick. We talk this matter over in private about convention and behold you have it. I vill go to it if possible." At my suggestion both Panizzi and Watts have promised to write to the Convention. I really wish some invitations had been sent over. Even now I think that you had better have some printed *very neatly* and sent to Trübner with directions to post at once and pay postage. Send him a list of such names as you deem best not only here but on the continent. . . . Of course you will see about securing a hall. Suppose you correspond with Jewett. The thing must not fall through now but be pushed so that it shall be a creditable affair. . . . Remember me kindly to Gilman and tell him to work hard for the Convention for it will make a mark.[38]

To his friend, Francis Haywood, Panizzi wrote:

There is going to be a Congress of librarians in the United States, which is to open on the 15th of September next, and where all the great questions connected with the management of a great library are to be discussed and uniform principles adopted. The Americans have always been my friends, and the principles which will prevail are mine. They wish me to go and I should like to amazingly, but the expense is too heavy. I will try, if possible, to get help from the Trustees. Do you think it possible, in case of my going, that if the packet is not full I might have a cabin to myself?[39]

But Sir Anthony, the picturesque and pugnacious Italian-born director of the British Museum who for years was the stormy petrel of every policy regarding Britain's great institution, did not get across. Whether duties prevented or whether he failed to get the hoped-for help from his trustees, we do not know. It would have added color and significance

25

to this first gathering of the craft if there could have been a delegate from overseas. James Yates, of Leeds, England, did come over to the meeting in 1876 at which the American Library Association was born,[40] and several American librarians went to London the following year and were present at the organization of the British association.[41] At many gatherings in the past seventy years on both sides of the Atlantic representatives from across the water have been present and have materially helped in promoting international understanding and good fellowship. I have had the good fortune myself to attend two library conferences in Great Britain and one on the continent, and the pleasure of helping to play the host to those who have come over to our side.

Norton's suggestion to Grant that he "correspond with Jewett" is a further reminder of the prominent part played by the latter in working up the Convention and in helping to carry it to a successful conclusion.

Writing to Grant from the National Hotel, Washington, probably in April of that Convention year, Norton said:

I have just returned from a long conversation with Prof. Jewett, the points of which I write down for fear my memory may prove treacherous. As regards the Convention he is decidedly and strongly in favor of it and at the time suggested, viz. the 15th of September. He says that if a call is drawn up and signed by Cogswell and Folsom he will also sign it, be on hand to take part and use such influence as may be in his power to forward its interest, but it is evident that he does not wish to appear prominent in the matter. If we can work upon Cogswell to put the ball rolling there are plenty to kick it. . . . Jewett is very much pleased with Poole's Index; spoke of it several times; says that it is sure to sell well.[42]

S. *Hastings Grant* to *Charles C. Jewett*[43]

MERCANTILE LIBRARY OF THE CITY OF NEW YORK
New York, August 13th, 1853

Prof. C. C. Jewett

DEAR SIR:

I have long been designing to write you but have not heard from you or learned your movements so I have not known exactly where to meet you. The time for the Libns Convention draws nigh, and it is important that some of the preliminaries shd be arranged, that when we organize, there may be no unnecessary delay. Doubtless your own views in reference to the manner of proceeding are already arranged but as I know not what they are, and as I have had to form some general ideas—I will merely make these known to you as addl data for concluding what will be the best mode of taking up matters.

Thursday, Sept. 15th is the day for meeting, and as our time must necessarily be short—it might be as well that we shd meet promptly say @ 10 or 12 o'clock. The room I will endeavor to have ready in some central position. Officers will of course have to be chosen and a comm. for that purpose ought to be all ready to report. Will you please designate the persons who shd compose such Comm. Committees wd then be in order on the several important subjects wh shd come up for consideration. As it is pretty generally understood who will constitute the more important part of the members present, (see call) wd it not be as well to designate the subjects most suited for consideration and have some person chosen on each, who would be well adapted to act as ch'man of such Comm. and let him be preparing himself on the subject, that a paper might be presented by such Comm. on the morning of the second day. To this end I have prepared a list of subjects wh might be considered—to which you will add, or you will modify. I have entered in part names opposite them— that your labors might be reduced. You will see that there is a large field laid out and you may not think it advisable that all shd be represented in Comm. but I considered it best to put down all, that you might the more readily decide wh shd be treated in this way and wh not. If papers on each subject are to be presented, the surest way of procuring them, wd be to have some one engaged beforehand to draw up his views thereon. Otherwise too much time might be wasted in such consideration.

You will not I hope think me too rash in presuming to do what I have done. It was necessary that some plan shd be adopted and I have merely endeavored to afford some material for your consideration. Will you not in an informal way inform such persons of your views and propose to them their coming somewhat prepared to represent such interests. No one wd probably hesitate when he feels that too much will not be expected under the circumstances and yet it will add much to the efficiency of the convention to have some such consideration previously given.

Be so kind as to write and give me suggestions as to what can be done here—the best way of doing it. I had purposed having invitations ready to visit the Great Exposition under favorable auspices and for seeing a few of our notable sights. There will also be one or two general evening receptions not confined exclusively to the members of the Convention for the purpose of becoming generally acquainted, etc. and a little more general bringing in such as sympathise with its objects. An early reply wd facilitate, as some things of importance are yet to be done—such as awaking the press, etc. Norton writes that in England there are many who look earnestly to this meeting who sympathise deeply in it.

As this *may* be the only Convention wh will be held here for some time extra effort shd be made by its friends.

Believe me, Dear Sir, to remain with deep respect, Yours,

S. HASTINGS GRANT

28

Charles C. Jewett to S. Hastings Grant[44]

WASHINGTON 16 Aug. 1853

MY DEAR SIR:

I received yesterday your letter of the 13th inst. and hasten to reply. I was very glad to hear from you respecting the librarians' convention, for I have of late felt considerable solicitude about it. Are we likely to have a respectable number present? And will those who come, be prepared to take an active part? We ought, perhaps, before calling the convention to have obtained positive promises from a sufficient number to have rendered it certain that the meeting would be spirited. Since the call was published, I have seen but very few who would be likely to take an interest in the convention. But I have found some, on whom I had counted, who seem unwilling to take any active part. The fact is our fraternity are generally very quiet, unostentatious men, not accustomed to public speaking, or fond of exhibiting themselves. Besides, our pursuits are not of such nature, as to reward our labors by brilliant discourses, or results that will resound in the busy world. We must work hard and long, with small visible effect, and in the track where hundreds, more learned than ourselves perhaps, have worked before us. More than all this, there are but few—very few—who have devoted themselves professsionally to bibliography. This taken up by the young man for a few years till he can "get something better to do" or assumed as an extra labor to eke out the income of some half paid professor.

But, notwithstanding all this, there are some among us, who feel a professional interest in the office of librarian; there are private gentlemen too, engrossed in other business it is true, but still finding time for the cultivation of bibliographical pursuits with great success. It is undeniable too that in our civilization, engrafted upon that of the old world and drawing thence and through that its sap, but spreading out into a more luxuriant growth than ever could have been attained by the parent tree, to yield richer and more abundant fruit—books and libraries are to assume and are assuming a new and more important function than ever before. But I need not say all this to you. I allude to it to show my own views respecting the convention, that though we may not be able to do much this year, we are starting in the right direction. The meeting this year cannot be a failure unless we raise expectations which we cannot meet. If but a dozen of us meet round a table to talk together over library economy for a day and concert measures for future meetings—it will be beneficial. But I hope that more can be done. Such things are generally started by a correspondence among those interested in the matter. Each agrees to be present and promises to do his part to make the occasion valuable and spirited. It has not been possible to do this to any great extent in the present case. I do not know how many you may have conferred with, or what may have been promised. I would have made more effort had it been in my power. But my private affairs have taken every moment of time that I could spare from official duties, and the latter have been, on account of the protracted sickness of my first assistant at the time when I most needed him doubly onerous. I cannot do much now. I will (Providence permitting) be present and contribute all that I can. I should like to bring forward, for a full and familiar discussion, my catalogue plan, or rather the "Smithsonian Catalogue System" as I prefer to call it. The second edition of the book which I printed last year is in press and I hope will be completed before the meeting.[45] This much enlarged and I hope improved. I have prepared as examples under the rules, the titles of all the bibliographical works in this Library. To these I hope soon to add those of the Astor Library, Brown University and the Boston Athenaeum, etc., and thus have a complete catalogue of all the bibliographical works in the country. To these I propose hereafter to add notes original and selected.

We are at work on the catalogues of the Library of Congress. Our force is 3 cataloguers, 2 compositors, 1 stereotyper and a boy to assist. The work is going bravely on notwithstanding the sickness of Mr. Corson on whose assistance I had so much relied. I hope to have a considerable number of titles to exhibit. The whole system is now fairly started and I am ready to have it talked about. I particularly wish to have it understood by the librarians. I want them, if they approve of it, to give me their countenance and support, for without them I can do nothing. To this end, I hope to have a familiar dicussion, where questions can be asked and doubts and difficulties suggested freely. I will send you the sheets of the books as they are worked off. This edition will be for the public and may therefore be spoken of openly. The last edition I published for private distribution and the criticism of friends.

If thought desirable I will also read an article on the Classification of books. I may also find among my long neglected papers something else which may do to read if it is desirable. But I hope others will occupy the time. I have no time for preparation.

It seems to me very desirable that some arrangements should be made beforehand, to prevent unnecessary delay after we meet. These arrangements can only be made by yourself and others in New York. Is Mr. Cogswell now in the city? Can you not consult with him and Mr. Moore and Mr. Fiske and Mr. Felt—Mr. Putnam perhaps. Mr. Norton will I hope be back in time to help and a most efficient helper he is too. Will Mr. Cogswell be present and will he accept the office of President? Either he or Mr. Folsom ought I think to hold the office. I have thought it might be well to address a circular to those supposed to be most interested in the matter, requesting them to inform you immediately whether they will be present, and also to send to you the title of any article which they may have to present and to name any topic which they would like to introduce for discussion. From the replies we should be able to judge what can be done and can quickly arrange a programme. The nominating committee, etc., can be selected informally the evening of the meeting. Written reports can hardly be expected at this session. The course of business will probably be to listen to such papers as may be offered and then to discuss the subject and if desired pass resolutions, refer to Committees, etc.

It would be very desirable to write to a few gentlemen, such as Mr. Folsom, Mr. Haven, Mr. Herrick, Mr. Livermore, Mr. Hale, etc., asking them to prepare a paper for presentation. I would do this if I could but I do not see how it is possible. The list of topics which you present is a very excellent one. Can you write to these gentlemen and get them to promise the papers. There is one other topic which I should like to bring forward if circumstances favor it—I mean that of a National Library of reference and research. I will write a form of circular which will show my views with reference to it.

You must not think it an assumption on your part to take these preliminary steps. Some one in New York must do it, or the whole thing will be a failure. If you and one or two others in New York will draw up a circular and send it to all librarians and others particularly interested in such matters, I have no doubt it will do more than anything else that can be done to promote the success of the enterprise. You may fall back upon me to any extent to back you up—only "go ahead!"

I have written very hastily and consequently with great prolixity not having time to condense. If anything else occurs to you that you wish to communicate with me about, I shall probably be here till the 14th Sept. and I will endeavor to answer your letters at once.

I remain, Most sincerely yours,

C. C. Jewett

S. H. Grant, Esq., N. Y.[46]

This letter to Grant shows well by inference the important part he played in laying out the general arrangements and in shaping up the details for the Convention. Grant's high regard for Jewett and his views and his deference to the somewhat older man are likewise apparent. The desire to

32

have Jewett take the lead and suggest procedure is clear and yet we suspect that Grant expected Jewett would defer to him and to Norton and would agree to approve their actions if only they would, as Jewett expressed it, "go ahead."

It seems clear from Jewett's letter that he did little toward actually working up the Convention, but his position and influence gave his suggestions weight, and because of his "primate" standing among American librarians his approval of steps taken was considered nothing short of necessary. This discursive letter of his tells us less about the projected Convention than we could wish, but incidentally it does give us a good picture of the status of the average American librarian of 1853—a man of small importance in his community, and so quiet and unostentatious that little public attention was paid to the work he was doing.

Jewett's heart and mind, his letter shows, was centered in his pet scheme, the hope of successfully sterotyping book titles for use in general library catalogs. He described this scheme in detail to the Convention at the morning session of its second day.

The original copy of "the list of topics" for possible discussion which Grant drew up and enclosed in his letter to Jewett has not been found but it was probably that printed in the *Gazette* for June 1853.[47] This too was undoubtedly the "matter to be talked about" referred to by Norton in his letter from London, written after his call on Panizzi.

This "Synopsis of Library Economy," as the *Gazette* headed it, was under three main divisions: (1) The Library: Its Character; (2) The Library Building: Points To Be Observed; and (3) Library Management.

The Library, in its character, it was pointed out, might be either reference or circulating, embodying the functions both of a reference and a circulating library; or special, as historical, natural science, medical, law, theology, or philological collections.

Among the points to be observed in the Library Building were: the architectural taste which should be displayed; the questions of proper light, heat, ventilation and security against fire; the division of the reading rooms into newspaper, periodical, and general study rooms; and the decision as to how far provision should be made for "lecture rooms, picture galleries, museums of natural history and curiosities, conversation rooms, rooms for instruction, wardrobes."

Library management listed a large part of those problems which have engaged the attention and thought of librarians from 1853 to the present time: the qualifications of the librarian, his previous training, his acquaintance with the manufacture and publishing of books, his familiarity with languages, his knowledge of kindred institutions, his requirements in the way of competent assistants, bibliographical works, and the hint that he should have leisure for study and "converse with literary men."

The Synopsis then went on to outline some of the important features of library work: the proper arrangement of books on the shelves, catalogs for the public and for the librarian, catalogs not only of printed books but of pamphlets, manuscripts and maps; the proper regulations for lending, the number of volumes allowed, the length of loan, penalty for damage, how "strangers" were to be allowed access to the library and reading rooms. Under Miscellanea such questions were raised as the best kinds of binding, registers of members and visitors, how to make suggestions for new books, and the times for closing, for cleaning, for taking an inventory, and for cataloging, evidently assuming that this latter procedure had to have its own time and season.

All in all the Synopsis is interesting to the librarian of a hundred years later. Its perusal gives one a remarkable feeling of kinship to these bibliothecal brethren of an earlier era who were even then struggling with so many problems all of which we are not yet sure have been satisfactorily solved.

No wonder Panizzi and Watts concluded it would take at least a month! But Hastings Grant and whoever else (Guild perhaps) may have had a hand in compiling the list, clearly did not expect *all* of these subjects and their ramifications to be disposed of at one convention. Rather, here was a menu from which the guests could select such dishes as they best liked. The advocates of the Convention feared, as voiced by Jewett, that the delegates would arrive without ideas for the program, and that, to assure success, ideas must be thrust before them.

An editorial in the August issue of *Norton's Literary Gazette,* written probably by Daniel Gilman, beats the tom-tom in a way similar to that by which a more modern library press has frequently aimed to awaken interest in the programs of American Library Association conferences.

As we have already intimated, there can be little doubt that our largest libraries will be represented at the Convention, by their librarians, managers, and friends. Their experience and skill will be of the greatest value to the public, while these gentlemen themselves are among the foremost to see that a comparison of views, one with another, will be greatly to the advantage of their several institutions. But this Convention is not alone for them. It is also intended for the directors of the smaller organizations, the numerous Young Men's Institutes, the School and

Society Libraries, which are scattered over our land, especially in New England and New York. We have some reason to fear that such persons will take less interest in this Convention than they should, and we, therefore, wish to express, in the most decided manner, our convictions, that a large attendance of Librarians from every part of our country, whatever the size of the institutions they represent, whether College, State, Social, Public, Mercantile, Mechanics', Young Men's, or School Libraries, will be of the greatest benefit to the various collections of books thus represented, and, through them, will be of lasting service to the literary advancement and the popular education of our countrymen.

The Convention will, of course, continue in session at least for two or three days. In that time, the views of men, eminent in various specialties, will be brought out, and he must be either very wise or very foolish, who does not receive many new hints, and learn many practical lessons. Mr. Jewett will be present, to set forth the position which the Smithsonian Institution is ready to hold for the advancement of libraries, and the publication of their catalogues. Dr. Cogswell, we doubt not, will impart many excellent suggestions from the experience he has employed and acquired, in collecting, so judiciously and so speedily, the largest and most valuable library of this country. Mr. Folsom, Mr. Livermore, Mr. Harris, and, we hope, Dr. Shurtleff, will be present to speak of those numerous and admirable collections of books for which Cambridge and Boston are famous. Mr. Barnard is to attend, and there is no one better than he to represent the academies and young men's institutes which are found in Southern New England. Mr. Herrick, we presume, will bring out of his varied stores of practical information many important facts and principles, and many others, more than we can mention, will contribute, either personally or in writing, suggestions, inquiries, statements, and reports which will not only be highly interesting but of lasting value.

The owners of private collections of books form another class of persons, who should, for their own sakes and that of the public, be well represented in the Convention. Many of these libraries, in particular departments of literature are among the most important in our country. Those of Mr. Lenox[48] and Mr. Livermore[49] in Bibles, of Mr. Salisbury [50] in Oriental works, of Mr. Force,[51] of Mr. Brown,[52] and others, in works on American History, occur to us at this moment. The Convention, as we understand it, is open to all thus interested in private collections of books, and not only so, but their presence and co-operation will be of the greatest value.[53]

It would have been truly a wonderful convention if even a half of Gilman's (if they were his) predictions and promises had come to pass! But so always has been the way of "advance agents."

Our surmise that this editorial was composed by Daniel Gilman is based on a note written by him to Guild from New Haven on August 10, just about the time copy for the August 15 number of the *Gazette* would be in preparation.

"I want to enlarge," Gilman wrote, "on Librarians' Convention as this is our last appearance before that assembly convenes. It seems to me that something rather def[inite] should be said about place of meeting—manner of proceeding, etc., as the time draws near to hand. Have you heard from Jewett?"[54]

Chapter Three

"IN ACCORDANCE WITH A CALL ISSUED IN MAY, 1853, SIGNED by various gentlemen interested in the management of public libraries, a number of librarians and other literary gentlemen convened at the smaller chapel of the University of the city of New York, at ten o'clock on Thursday morning, Sept. 15th, 1853."

So reads the opening paragraph of the Proceedings as printed · in the October number of *Norton's Literary Gazette*.[55] The abridged and abbreviated record here reproduced of this first known meeting of librarians has drawn on both the *Gazette* and *Norton's Literary and Educational Register, for 1854*.[56] The account in the former was hastily thrown together in the three or four weeks immediately following the Convention and contains some errors which were corrected in the fuller and more carefully prepared report in the *Register*, which came out in December. The *Gazette* gives what was apparently the order in which the various items of business were transacted, and this order is here followed with a few exceptions. The *Register*, issued some two months later, records in full some addresses and reports which were merely summarized in the *Gazette*. It has not seemed necessary to distract the reader's attention by stating from which of these two sources each particular piece of business is derived.

The Proceedings were, naturally, the work chiefly of the secretary, S. Hastings Grant, but he was ably assisted by his friend, Reuben A. Guild, as correspondence between them shows. Daniel Gilman doubtless helped as far as he was able; but in December, as we have already reported, he, in company with his friend, Andrew D. White, sailed for Europe and was consequently, perhaps we may assume, too busy getting ready for his journey to devote much time to editorial details.

Charles Folsom, the fifty-nine-year-old head of the Boston Athenaeum, called the assembly to order and, after a few explanatory remarks, read the Call. The *New York Daily Tribune* said the next morning:

The quiet diffidence of the study seemed to have accompanied these literary Treasurers, and it was some time before their proceedings took a definite form, each appearing to prefer a whispering consultation with his neighbor, to the more formal proceedings of appointing President and organizing Business Committees. Ultimately, Mr. Charles Folsom, being the oldest librarian present, was requested by the delegates to open the Convention.

Folsom stated that the meeting would be of such an informal character that only a very simple organization would be needed and proposed that a president and secretary be chosen.

In the course of a two-and-a-half columns account of the first day's business, the *New York Daily Times,* of September 16, stated that "Mr. Folsom was requested to act as Chairman, but declined." Of this the official Proceedings have nothing to say, but rather that, on motion of Guild, Charles Coffin Jewett was unanimously elected President. Then Folsom, released from the chair, moved the election of Seth Hastings Grant as Secretary, and this was unanimously done.

39

A little later a committee "to prepare and arrange the business of the Convention" was appointed to consist of Charles Folsom, Philip J. Forbes, of the New York Society Library, J. W. Wallace, of the Philadelphia Law Association, Reuben A. Guild, of Brown University, R. H. Stephenson, of the Cincinnati Mercantile Library, together with the President and Secretary of the Convention.

Jewett, on taking the chair, acknowledged the honor conferred upon him, and proceeded to comment upon the objects of the Convention, and to state the means by which these ends could be accomplished. His remarks on that occasion were probably incorporated by him in the draft he prepared for publication of the address he delivered later in that morning's session. There seems to have been no stenographer present at any of the meetings and the remarks made by Jewett were printed in the *Register* from copy later submitted by him, based on what he actually said, so far as he could recall his words. Possibly more recent conference speeches have been "corrected" in a similar manner! His address is here given in full because we believe it, as the first presidential address at a library convention, deserves our attention and commands our interest.

JEWETT'S PRESIDENTIAL ADDRESS

It must be highly gratifying to those who signed the call for this Convention, to notice the response which it, this morning, receives. To every one who knows the nature of a librarian's duties,—the details which consume his days, and render absence from his post impossible, except at the cost of severe labor on his return,—it must be manifest that we have met at considerable personal sacrifice. We obey some strong and wide-felt impulse in incurring the expense and the trouble of this gathering.

The call for this Convention was not the result of a correspondence among librarians, nor was it the subject of long and careful consideration. It was, rather, a spontaneous movement. It was first, I think, suggested a year ago, or more, in the *Literary Gazette*. Librarians spoke to each other on the matter, when they happened to meet. Every one was pleased with the idea. At length a formal call was written, and signed by a few who happened to meet the gentlemen having charge of the paper.

In compliance with such an invitation, we have assembled this morning. It is not, so far as I know, proposed to accomplish any end by this Convention, beyond the general one expressed in the call, of "conferring together upon the means of advancing the prosperity and usefulness of public libraries," and of seeking mutual instruction and encouragement in the discharge of the quiet and unostentatious labors of our vocation, for which each, at his separate post, finds perhaps but little sympathy—for which each, when at home, must derive enthusiasm only from within himself, and from the silent masters of his daily communion.

We have no peculiar views to present, no particular set of measures to propose. We meet without preparation. No order of business has been arranged. Our proceedings must be spontaneous as our meeting. It is not important that they be systematic and formal. We come to receive and to act upon suggestions. We are not here for stately debate, much less for an exhibition of ourselves. These things are foreign from our vocation, and not congenial with our tastes. We meet for familiar, informal, conversational conference, where each may take his part, and no one be prevented from contributing his share to the profits of the enterprise, by his inexperience in public speaking, or his inability to make elaborate preparation. Those gentlemen connected with the public press who honor us with their presence, must have been attracted hither by a scholarlike sympathy with our quiet pursuits, which will lead them to appreciate our feelings in this respect, in the reports which they may give.

It is indeed to be hoped that our meeting will have its influence upon the public mind. If our discussions are natural and unrestrained, suggested and shaped by right views of the position which we hold, or ought to hold, in general society and in the republic of letters; if they present to ourselves and to others the difficulties with which we have to contend; if they elicit thought and information upon the collecting of books for private culture, for public enlightenment, and for learned investigations, and upon the best means of promoting the increase and efficiency of such collections;—if we manifest here, while we talk of books as material objects, and of books in their internal significance, that respectful, dignified, and noiseless spirit inspired by the associations in the midst of which we live, the public will certainly feel and acknowledge the beneficial influence of our meeting, and will desire an official report of the progress and results of our deliberations.

The occasion is one of peculiar interest. This is the first convention of the kind, not only in this country, but, so far as I know, in the world.

There have, indeed, been bibliographical associations, but they have been, for the most part, composed of *dilettante,* and not of practical librarians and lovers of books. The gratification of a passion for rare and curious books has generally been their object. Books were too often valuable to them, only as they were worthless to the rest of the world. Each member glorying in the possession of a unique copy of some old work, was required to reprint it, with only copies enough to give one to each member. One society has played the part of *bibliotaph* by requiring, that if a member dies, and his copy of one of these reprints is to be sold by auction, it shall be bought by the Society at any price it may be necessary to pay.

These associations have had their origin in a different state of society from ours. We can at present have but little sympathy with their principal design. We have none whatever with their selfishness.

We would not be supposed to chide the passion for book rarities, where it exhibits itself simply in collecting and preserving what is curious and costly, and not in its destruction or concealment. Why should not a rich man spend his money in this way, as well as in a thousand others which are harmless? We may go further, and assert that a collection of rare books can scarcely be formed, without subserving the interests of learning, whether made with such a design or not. The public are not unfrequently surprised by results anticipated only by the collector.

I may allude, in this connection, to a distinguished gentleman in our own country, who made, at great expense, a collection of early-printed books, without any regard to the subjects of which they treated, the languages in which they were written, or their worth as literary productions. By those who did not know his purpose, he was called a *bibliomaniac*. He had, however, a definite object in view, which was, to investigate the early history of typography by its monuments. Books which he never cared to read, were full of instruction to him. He deduced from the close examination of them, many facts new to the bibliographical world, and showed the unsoundness of many generally received theories. For example, he satisfied himself that books, in the early days of typography, were never printed from block letters, that is, from separate types of wood, or of wood faced with metal. He proved, too, that many of these books were printed one page at a time. It had been supposed that the early printers must have had immense fonts of type. In many folios the sheets are quired, and it was very naturally supposed that the type of every page of the quire must have been set up before any was printed off. But he traced a broken letter from page to page, and he found such irregularities of register as could not have occured, had the two pages of the same form been printed at the same time; and he thus demonstrated that these books were printed page by page, and that consequently only a very small font of type was necessary.

Now, these are new, interesting, and valuable results; and they are only specimens which occur to me at the moment, of deductions from the examination of books, which an ordinary observer would say it was infatuation to collect.

But our object, at present, is of a more manifestly and eminently practical and utilitarian character. We meet to provide for the diffusion of a knowledge of good books, and for enlarging the means of public access to them. Our wishes are for the public, not for ourselves.

In our assembling today we obey the impulses of our peculiar civilization. We are preeminently a reading people. In Prussia the whole population are taught to read; but a distinguished citizen of that country, who had traveled in the United States, once expressed to me the difference between his own countrymen and the Americans, by saying: "Our people *can* read, your people *do* read." The generally diffused love of reading, for the sake of gaining information, has led to the establishment of a large number of libraries, so that, in the number and general diffusion of small collections of books, we are richer already than any other country in the world. Reading creates the desire to read more, and select reading increases the desire to read profitably. Hence, in every village the questions are asked: "How shall we get good books? How shall we keep them? How shall we use them?" To consult on the best replies to questions like these, is one of the objects of our assembling today.

Another demand of our peculiar civilization is, for the means of thorough and independent investigation. We wish to own no men as masters. We intend to re-examine all history from our own American stand point, and we must rewrite it, where we find its facts have been tortured to teach the doctrines of injustice and oppression. The mental activity of this country is surveying every field of research, literary, scientific, aesthetic, industrial, and philanthropic. It requires to know what others have done and thought, that it may itself press farther outward. This country,

44

therefore, demands the means of the amplest research, and this demand must and will be met.

These views have impressed themselves deeply upon our minds, as we are the appointed custodians of the literary treasures of the country, and have led us to desire mutual assistance and concentration of efforts in providing for these intellectual necessities of our American life. For our present meeting it has been proposed to adopt the simplest form of organization; to appoint, besides a president and a secretary, a business committee to receive suggestions and propositions, and arrange the order of proceedings for each day's session. I unite most cordially in the hope which I have heard expressed this morning, that this Convention may be the precursor of a permanent and highly useful association.[57]

Reuben Guild, writing of Jewett nearly twenty-five years later, said: "I can never forget the impression which the elegance of his person, the refinement of his manners, his pleasant voice, his kindly smile, his beaming eyes, his cordial affection for his friends, and his urbanity towards all, made upon my mind. It is clear and distinct to this day."[58]

At the close of this address Secretary Grant, at the chair's suggestion, read the names of the gentlemen present, who rose and identified themselves as their names were called. The names of the eighty-two delegates who constituted the personnel of the Convention are printed in an Appendix.[59]

Letters were then read from several librarians apologizing for their unavoidable absence: Edward C. Herrick,[20] of Yale, T. Romeyn Beck,[60] of the New York State Library, B. P. Johnson,[61] of the New York Agricultural Society, Adolph Frost,[62] of Burlington (N. J.) College Library, and William MacDermott,[63] of Norristown, Pa.

"The first term of our Collegiate year," Yale's librarian wrote from New Haven on September 14, "commences today.

45

My engagements are consequently so pressing at this time that I cannot leave home, and I shall thus be unavoidably deprived of the pleasure and profit of attending the Convention of Librarians to be held in New York tomorrow.

"I feel great interest in the matters to be discussed at the Convention, and very much regret to lose the advantages to be derived from attendance.

"Should there be any assessment on the members my friend Mr. D. C. Gilman will pay in my behalf."[64]

So far as preserved records show there was no assessment on the delegates. There must have been at least a few incidental expenses; perhaps Charles B. Norton assumed them; perhaps the hat was informally passed.

Folsom read part of a letter from George Livermore, Boston business man, prominent at that time in antiquarian and bibliographical circles, regretting his detention. He apologized for the absence also of Dr. Cogswell,[34] of the Astor Library, Dr. Harris,[19] librarian of Harvard, and Dr. Sears,[23] of the Massachusetts State Library, explaining that they were all kept away by pressing engagements. On behalf of Dr. Cogswell he presented an invitation to visit the Astor Library at four o'clock on Friday afternoon, and the invitation was accepted. The official Proceedings make no mention of the visit, but the *Times* on Saturday morning reported that the business committee, in its arrangements of Friday's activities scheduled a visit to the Astor Library at four, "members to leave the University at $3\frac{1}{2}$ P.M." Later in the same article the *Times* recorded: "After adjourning the members proceeded to the Astor Library, Lafayette Place, where they were received by Dr. Cogswell. They were all much pleased with the appearance of the building and its valuable contents." The reason for Cogswell's absence from the sessions of the Convention has already been given, namely, that his time was fully occupied in preparing to open the Astor Library at an early date.[65]

Invitations to visit various other libraries were presented at that Thursday morning session from: the New York Society, the New York Historical Society, Union Theological Seminary, Columbia College, the Mercantile, the American Institute, the Mechanics' Institute, and the Free Academy. Other invitations extended were from the directors of the Crystal Palace Industrial Exposition, the city's "big show" of the year, from the Gallery of Christian Art,[66] from Dr. Henry Abbott's Museum of Egyptian Antiquities[67] and from John Banvard to visit his Panorama of the Holy Land, at 596 Broadway.[68]

These polite invitations were politely received and acknowledged but, having some knowledge of the demands on the time of conference members, we doubt if all of them were availed of, although most of the delegates probably took advantage of the privilege of seeing the famous Astor Library on Friday afternoon.

With more particularity "Notice was also given that members of the Convention, resident in the city, would be happy to receive, in a social manner, the members of the Convention from abroad and other invited guests, at the Kemble House, No. 45 East Nineteenth Street, on Friday evening, from 8 to 11 o'clock." No further reference to this affair appears in the Proceedings, but, again from the press, we know that the reception was held.

The *Times* reported the next morning:

An excellent dinner was provided and the members enjoyed themselves highly. The walls were decorated with portraits of our

47

most distinguished authors, and on the tables were displayed various illustrated works and rare books.

Said the *Herald:*

We observed among other books which were lying in the reception room an old copy of the Psalms of David, belonging to the Loganian Library of Philadelphia. It was a manuscript copy, but was so neatly executed in imitation of print that it easily deceived a person at first sight. It was also illuminated with great taste, and, take it altogether, it was one of the greatest literary curiosities we have ever seen. It bore date 1400, just previous to the invention of types. There was also a copy of "Poor Richard's Almanac" from the year 1733 to 1747. It was printed "by Benjamin Franklin at the new printing office, near the Market, Philadelphia."

To encounter fourteenth-century manuscripts and Franklin imprints was possibly outside the daily experience of the *Herald's* reporter.

To return to Thursday morning: After these various invitations to visit local institutions had been presented, Charles B. Norton expressed the interest felt by European librarians regarding the Convention which he had discovered in the course of his summer trip and stated that some communications entrusted to him would be presented at a "future hour." "This movement in America," Norton said, "had incited the librarians of England generally to desire a similar opportunity of conferring together on matters of a kindred nature to those which drew this Convention together."[69]

At this point the Rev. Samuel Osgood, a delegate from the Providence Athenaeum, arose and addressed the chair.

"I suppose, Mr. President," said he, "that no business is

at present formally before the Convention, and that it is in order for any member to suggest topics of interest for the consideration of the [business] committee just chosen."

Samuel Osgood had been a Unitarian minister in Providence but had, a short time before, removed to New York and had become the pastor of the Church of the Messiah on Broadway. He was an able man and influential in many circles. In 1869, when he was fifty-seven years old, he left the Unitarian fellowship and entered the ministry of the Protestant Episcopal Church.[70] He was, by the way, the father of Mabel Osgood Wright, author of a number of popular works on natural history, and in her book, *My New York,* in which she writes of her girlhood in that city, she gives pleasing glimpses of her father, of their strolls together and of poking into out-of-the-way and little known corners of the old town. In Providence Osgood had been a trustee of the Providence Athenaeum and that already venerable institution had appointed him as its delegate to the Librarians' Convention, in addition to its librarian, Thomas Hale Williams, and Albert J. Jones, one of the trustees.

The address[71] which Samuel Osgood then proceeded to deliver on that morning, nearly a hundred years ago, is of historical interest to library-minded folk of this generation, for in that day, long before the establishment of state library commissions, county libraries, or other agencies for library extension, he made a well-composed plea for library service to small towns and communities, a plea for what he termed "popular libraries," meaning by that phrase very much what we mean by "public" libraries, except that neither in his address nor in any other business of the 1853 Convention was there a hint or suggestion of tax support for the proposed and recommended libraries. It was the era of subscription libraries, young men's lyceums, mercantile and mechanics' libraries, and, for the upper stratum of society, the athenaeum and the society library.

Charles C. Jewett, in the introductory remarks to his *Report on the Public Libraries of the United States,* published in 1850, expresses in these words the sense in which the term "public libraries" was there used by him: "Libraries which are accessible—either without restriction, or upon conditions with which all can easily comply—to every person who wishes to use them for their appropriate purposes."[72] In 1853 there were about 700 libraries in the United States,—mercantile, society, school and college—possessing an aggregate of about 2,000,000 volumes, amidst a total population of approximately 25,000,000 people.

After a few pleasant and appropriate remarks concerning the occasion and the object which had brought them together, a graceful compliment to their presiding officer, "who has done such eminent service to the library cause in this country;" and taking care not to appear lacking in appreciation of the importance of strengthening the university and other scholarly libraries of the land, Osgood launched upon the subject, "Popular Libraries," to which he had addressed himself.

I should be very glad at the fitting time to say my poor word in behalf of the highest class of public libraries, and the need of bringing them up to a more adequate standard. Proud as we are of our four or five great libraries, there is not one of them, not even that of Harvard University, my own cherished Alma Mater, that affords the requisite means for the thorough study of any one topic of recondite learning, even if of practical science. Any scholar who tries to investigate any ancient or historical subject will find, to his regret, that no library in the country has a plummet that can sound its depths. What facilities the noble Astor Library may afford, we can judge better when its merits are known and its treasures are consolidated.

There is no reason for being down-hearted at this state of things, for we cannot expect soon to rival the great libraries of Europe, and our present task is rather with the increase and improvement of libraries for the people, than with great central institutions such as the wealth of centuries only can endow. As the mass of the people obtain a higher culture by means at hand in every town and city, the demand for the highest class of books will increase, and the hope of national collections will brighten. Now what shall prevent our America from leading all nations of the earth *longo intervallo* in the number and value of our Popular Institutes and Athenaeums? We are probably not much behind, if at all behind, any portion of Europe in the number of books collected in our villages, and available to the community at large. But not a tithe of the progress has been made that should have been made. What prevents every community of a thousand inhabitants from having its well-chosen library of a thousand volumes? And if this ratio were to be carried out in all our towns, how vast would be the increase and how noble the triumph of a sound popular literature! May not this Convention do something, by its discussions and action, to call attention to this matter, and rouse many a slumbering township to its imperative duty? Who shall presume to estimate adequately the advantages coming from the establishment of a good library in a community not before so favored. The immediate vicinity and the whole nation share in the benefit. Many a thriving town needs some such centre of generous and elevating interest as an attractive library must be, and it should be considered but half civilized until such a centre is established. . . . The village library attracts to itself every congenial ally, and tends to diffuse social refinement as well as intellectual light. . . .

This Convention will not meet in vain, if it shall give the

51

incentive to form one new institution of the kind anywhere in the land. Every such library tends to foster a worthy public spirit among citizens of ample means. Many a successful merchant of the city, who has thriven largely in some "sugar trade or cotton line," and who abounds far more in generous impulses than literary attainments, would rejoice to send to his native town or village some choice work of art, or valuable selection of books, as a token of kindly remembrance, if an institution existed that should suggest the hint and indicate the method to the benefactor. It will be found that every well organized popular library has been much enriched by such donations. . . .

The whole country grows by such institutions, for they at once collect the local and fugitive literature, so important to the natural history, and they create a demand for the best class of books, securing of themselves an encouraging market for a good sized edition of every work of undoubted value. I call your attention seriously to the value of such enterprises, and urge you to do something to extend and improve them. . . . Where is the town of any importance that should not at once have its thousand of good books circulating among its people, and what but the want of the true spirit shall prevent our two millions of volumes from swelling to twenty millions, nay, reaching before the year of the next census the full limit of our numerical population, although it may exceed thirty millions? Sir, with your leave, I offer the following resolutions:

Resolved, That while we maintain most decidedly the importance of libraries of the highest class, in furtherance of the most advanced literary and scientific studies, and rejoice in the rise and progress of our few great collections of books for professional scholars, we are convinced that for the present our chief hope must be in the establishment and improvement of *popular* libraries throughout the land.

Resolved, That the Business Committee be requested to call attention to the desirableness of a popular Library Manual, which shall embody the most important information upon the chief points in question, especially upon—

1. The best organization of a Library society, in regard to its officers, laws, funds, and general regulations.

2. The best plans for Library edifices, and the arrangements of the shelves and books, with the requisite architectural drawings.

3. The most approved method of making out and printing catalogues.

4. The most desirable principle to be followed in the selection and purchase of books, as to authors and editions; with lists of such works as are best suited for libraries of various sizes, from 500 to 1,000 volumes or upwards.

Resolved, That the Business Committee be requested to consider the expediency of memorializing Congress to procure the preparation of such a Manual, through the agency of the Smithsonian Institution.

How warmly would Samuel Osgood, and others of that 1853 group, have welcomed Dana's *Library Primer,* or Lutie Stearns's *Essentials in Library Administration,* or some of the more recent publications of the American Library Association! But the time had not come. The agitations of these pioneers, however, were laying the foundations for later accomplishments.

Chapter Four

NO IMMEDIATE ACTION WAS TAKEN ON OSGOOD'S RESOLUTIONS, but at its last session, on Saturday morning, the Convention reverted to them, unanimously adopted them, and appointed a committee consisting of Osgood, Jewett and Guild to "take action" and report at the next meeting.[73]

There was good reason apparently for appointing Reuben Guild a member of this committee, for as far back as December 15, 1851, *Norton's Literary Advertiser*,[74] the earlier name for the *Gazette*, had announced as in preparation "a Librarian's and Book-Buyer's Manual, intended as a complete guide for the Formation, Arrangement, Preservation, and Proper Management of Libraries, both Public and Private." It would be a volume of about 500 pages, octavo, the announcement went on to say, embracing the principles of "Bibliography, Libraryography, Typography," etc.

A month later, January 15, 1852, *Norton's Literary Gazette*,[75] as the publication then began to be called, made a more extensive announcement, stating that they were now able to name the author and the publisher and to give further particulars of its plan.

Mr. Reuben A. Guild, Librarian of Brown University, has been preparing such a work. It will contain, so far as is possible, in addition to all the details pertaining to books, libraries, librarians, &c., a brief and accurate history of the origin and progress of printing, mechanism of the Art, &c.; a brief history of the libraries of the Ancients, statistics of modern libraries, both at home and abroad; a *complete* list of bibliographical works, and also a *select* list for small or private libraries; a general plan for the division and classification of books, and also an abridged plan for small or private libraries; a list of rare and curious books, together with a treatise on the same; principles which should govern in the selection of books, choice of editions, &c. . . .

The proprietor of this paper has made arrangements for publishing the book, in the best style, and it may be expected to be a valuable and permanent work of reference upon the subjects of which it treats.

Further notices and advertisements of the Manual appeared in the *Gazette* from time to time previous to the Convention. In May and June, 1852, Norton advertised the work as "in press," and in January, 1853, announced that he "will publish soon" Guild's Handbook for Librarians.

But the book did not appear and had not appeared when the resolution presented by Osgood was adopted by the Convention. Both Guild and Norton were presumably in the room when Osgood proposed his resolution and when the Convention adopted it, but, so far as the Proceedings show, neither made any statement about the work announced as forthcoming, nor did any delegate who may have seen the announcements in the *Gazette* refer to it.

There has been speculation over the years as to why this book, which Norton plainly announced as "in press" in 1852, was never published, for the projected work containing the features detailed in the *Gazette* announcement is quite different from Guild's *Librarian's Manual*, published in 1858. The manual, as published, contained 304 pages, instead of "about 500," was divided into two parts, the first

55

containing a list of 495 bibliographical works, arranged under various heads, some of which titles, but not all, were annotated; and the second part consisting of sketches of fourteen public, state, college, and university libraries in the United States and Europe. Important bibliographically and useful bibliothecally as the book doubtless was, it can readily be seen that it is quite another work from that announced by Norton as forthcoming in 1851 and 1852. It was not, by the way, issued by Norton, who by that time had met with financial reverses and gone out of the publishing business, but by Joel Munsell, of Albany, who tried to make it an exceptionally fine piece of typography, with thick paper and wide margins.

Why was Guild's *Manual,* as originally planned and actually "in press" in 1852, if we can take literally the *Gazette* announcements, withdrawn and so fundamentally changed when it was published nearly six years later? The probable reason why it was not issued along lines so fully outlined in the *Gazette* of January 15, 1852, quoted above, is found in an announcement in the *Gazette* of February 1, 1854.[76]

Nearly a year ago in view of the Convention of Librarians then about to be held in this city, we hastily sketched and published an outline of what we termed "Library Economics"; or, matters pertaining to the proper arrangement of a public collection of books. As no work then existed in our own language giving practical instruction upon this important subject, although one had been announced as in preparation, it was thought that the consideration of some of these topics upon that occasion would have an immediate and practical value. Such, we believe, was the case, although it was impossible that much attention should be given to minor details at this, the first meeting of the Association.

So perhaps we are forced to the conclusion that Guild's book was not "in press" in 1852, but had in reality only reached the stage where an outline of its expected contents was "hastily sketched and published." The *Gazette* went on to say

Recently, this field has been more fully entered upon by Mr. Edward Edwards, principal librarian of the Manchester Athenaeum, England, and the results given in the following prospectus of a Library Manual which he has announced for publication. Mr. Edwards' former connection with the British Museum, and his present position at the head of the most flourishing of the free libraries of Great Britain, has given him an intimate acquaintance with this whole subject, which is sufficiently evinced by the minuteness of his details.

Then follow in the *Gazette* two-and-a-half columns, outlining the contents of the projected work. The book was published in two volumes by Trüber, in London, in 1859, with the title, *Memoirs of Libraries: including a Handbook of Library Economy.*

The section called "Economy of Libraries" covers pages 567-1072 of the second volume. The chapters vary considerably in nature from the announcement in *Norton's Literary Gazette,* but no more so than might be expected from an outline released five years before the actual appearance of the book. This well-nigh exhaustive treatment of the subject might with good reason have caused Guild and his publisher to reach the conclusion that another book along the same lines would be neither expedient nor profitable, and that if Guild were to publish a Librarian's Manual at all it would need to be basically different from Edwards's announced work, and different from the announcements of

57

his own book made in the early years of that decade.

Why Osgood, in his resolution, suggested that Congress be memorialized to procure the publication of the Manual and that it be issued through the agency of the Smithsonian Institution we cannot say. Not being a librarian and perhaps not a reader of *Norton's Literary Gazette* he may not have known that Norton was proposing to publish Guild's book. But that, we think, is unlikely. He may have felt that the Manual would have greater weight and prestige if issued by order of Congress and through the agency of the Smithsonian, which, because of Jewett's position and influence, was the clearing house for so many current library ideas.

When the Rev. Mr. Osgood had concluded his address and introduced his resolutions, Lloyd P. Smith, librarian of the Philadelphia Library Company, addressed the chair, and, after concurring with Osgood's views, expressed the hope that the attention of Congress would be called to the importance of more thoroughly and judiciously distributing the public documents to the libraries of the country. At the afternoon session of the second day Smith, in whose mind a plan for improved distribution had apparently been working itself out, presented the following resolution:

WHEREAS, The documents published by order of the Congress of the United States, are printed in large numbers at the public expense, and

WHEREAS, It is desirable that they should be so distributed as to be accessible for reference to all citizens, and at the same time preserved for posterity, therefore,

Resolved, That a Committee of two be appointed to memorialize Congress, on behalf of this Convention, requesting the passage of a joint resolution, granting to the Smithsonian Institution, for distribution among the principal Public Libraries throughout the United States, copies of all such Journals of Congress, Senate Documents, House Documents, Reports of Committees, and other State Papers as may hereafter be printed by order of Congress.

After reading his resolution Smith proceeded to speak to it at some length. It was unnecessary, he said, for him to expatiate on the importance of the public documents and state papers. They were constantly wanted for reference, not only by historians, but by lawyers, claimants on the Government, and citizens generally, seeking information. In a word they were invaluable.

These documents were printed, he pointed out, at vast public expense, but by the present mode of distribution to members of Congress and to a few favored libraries only, they became, soon after publication, practically valueless because of their scarcity. After referring to an appropriation of $150,000, made shortly before, for a work which, it was supposed, would be a history of the Indian tribes,[77] Smith expressed the opinion that the money could better have been used in building up, on the foundation of the Library of Congress, or that of the Smithsonian Institution, a great National Library, which should be for this country what the British Museum, the Bibliothèque du Roi, the Royal Library of Berlin, and other national institutions are for the scholars of the old world.

As to the method of distributing documents recommended in his resolution, he felt that if at least three hundred copies of all public documents were handed over to the Regents of the Smithsonian Institution, they would be discreetly distributed to such libraries as would use them for the greatest benefit of the country.

Edward Everett Hale said he was very glad to see this

matter presented, as he looked upon it as "the most important subject that could be brought before them." The Government of the United States, he said, did more for the encouragement of literature than any government of the world, but through some mistake at Washington the documents printed at public expense were not distributed and circulated as generally as they ought to be; that a complete collection could not be found anywhere.

The resolution was unanimously adopted, and Lloyd Smith and Charles Folsom were appointed the committee. President Jewett was subsequently added. This committee was one of the few of the many named at the 1853 Convention which tried to "follow through" and discharge the duty laid upon it. In the December (1853) number of *Norton's Literary Gazette*[78] appears the draft of the proposed memorial to Congress, drawn up by Chairman Smith, requesting that at least three hundred copies of the documents designated in the resolution be transmitted to the Smithsonian for distribution by it to the principal libraries of the country. Smith asked "secretaries of literary institutions and others" to forward their names to some member of the committee that they might be added to the memorial. The committee was not, we fear, supported in this worthy undertaking, for no such memorial appears actually to have reached Congress; but the attempt of the Librarians' Convention to bring about a more effective and efficient distribution of public documents shows the venerable age of this troublesome problem, which has not even yet been settled to the entire satisfaction of everybody.

At this point, President Jewett delivered an address which, in the *Register,* was combined, as we have stated, with the remarks he made on taking the presiding officer's chair.

The Rev. Mr. Osgood then proposed that delegates relate "any special experience" in the working of their own libraries, and the remainder of that morning session and all of the afternoon session was devoted to oral reports made, more or less without previous preparation, by librarians representing various institutions from the New England states to St. Louis and New Orleans. The facts and figures presented were printed as a part of the Proceedings in the October *Gazette*. These reports and those from a considerably larger number of libraries were gathered and published in *Norton's Literary and Educational Register, for 1854*. Although they were incorporated in the *Gazette* and so became a part of the official Proceedings it has not seemed essential to reproduce them here. One is impressed with the meagre incomes, the small number of volumes, and, for the college libraries, the limited open hours.

The Harvard library, for example, was open only from 9 to 1 and 2 to 4; Yale from 10 to 1 and 3 to 5; Brown from 9 to 1; Princeton open only on Mondays and Tuesdays from 12 to 1. With such hours in force, reference service as we know it could not have been extensive or frequent. The idea of research had hardly reached the American university. The college library was open chiefly for the occasional loan of a book to a professor or student or the occasional perusal of the recent periodicals.

On the other hand, the hours of the young men's institutes, mercantile, and mechanics' libraries, were long—for the most part all day and until 9 or 10 at night. The Boston Mercantile Library, over which William F. Poole then presided, kept its reading room open "from 6½ A.M. until 10 P.M.," although its library proper kept the more moderate hours of 1 to 10. The New York Mercantile Library was open from 10 to 10. The aristocratic Boston Athenaeum reported 9 to 6, and the flexible Providence Athenaeum reported that "in the summer the library is open from 9 A.M. until sunset; in the winter, from 10 A.M. to 10 P.M."

Few of the mercantile or mechanics' libraries possessed over twenty thousand volumes; some less than ten thousand; a few even less than five. The New York Mercantile, by contrast, loomed large with nearly forty thousand volumes and a circulation in 1852 of 120,000. The circulation of books in these "popular" libraries, as a matter of fact, seems encouragingly large in proportion to the number of books owned and the extremely inadequate support.

During the presentation of these reports on that Thursday morning, Captain Henry Coppée,[79] the handsome, dapper thirty-two-year-old assistant professor of French at West Point, and, quite incidentally, the Academy's librarian, spoke of the poor support given to the library by the Government, only a thousand dollars a year being appropriated for the purchase of books. Coppée, like so many other members of that 1853 Convention, had a distinguished career. He was the son of a Santo Domingo physician who had fled the island on the outbreak of a slave rebellion and settled in Savannah, Georgia, where son Henry was born. Young Coppée graduated from West Point, went through the Mexican War with distinction and returned to the Military Academy to teach French. As a minor and unimportant additional duty he was placed in charge of the library, but Coppée was literary minded and took that job seriously. Said he, in addressing the Convention:

. . . You have read the *Medecin malgré lui*;[80] I may truly say that when I was appointed Librarian of the Military Academy,

I was a librarian in spite of myself. The little service I had seen, and the partial fondness for certain kinds of reading, had given me no knowledge of the great progressive science of bibliography, a science nobler in its results than simple authorship, in that it classifies and makes available at one intelligent glance, masses of matter, rich specimens of mental ore, which otherwise would lie hidden and useless to the world.

What, however, was received with reluctance, has been retained with pleasure, and pursued with such ardor as the pressure of other duties would permit. . . .

When the appointment of Librarian was conferred upon me, I found that, with a rigor at once ill-judged and ill-productive, almost all light literature—poetry, fiction and some of those charming modern works, which, verily, can only be characterized as lying between the two—a delectable land of the heart and the imagination—had been interdicted. Since that time, careful additions of standard works of these classes have been made: we ventured, sir, upon a set of the Waverley Novels, and introduced the Corps of Cadets to the Great Magician—need I add, with perfect satisfaction to all concerned.

I have one word to add in favor of a popular direction to our proceedings. It is in accordance with the pervading spirit of our government. The people, sir, are the rule; everything else, the exception.

Let our deliberations, then, not lose sight of this fact. Rare books cost great prices, and are read afterwards by few—the scholars, the great book-makers for future generations—and these should not be neglected; but, first remember, that good correct learning and knowledge, facts and practical science for the millions are within reach of small sums, the assessment of which will scarcely be felt by the poorest, and the aggregate of which will astonish the people by its greatness, and enlighten the world by its influence.

In 1855 Coppée resigned from the army and took the chair

of English literature and history in the University of Pennsylvania. Eleven years later he became the first president of Lehigh University. In addition to success in the educational field he was the author of several books on historical and literary subjects which were popular in their day.

Captain Coppée was not the only member of the Convention who was "a librarian in spite of himself." Most of the college and university librarians there operated their libraries as a side issue, teaching being their chief occupation. We have noted that Harris, of Harvard, and Herrick, of Yale, were better known as professors of entomology than as librarians; A. J. Upson was professor of rhetoric at Hamilton College as well as librarian; George M. Giger, librarian of the College of New Jersey—Princeton to us—was also professor of Greek, and Howard Crosby was professor of Greek as well as librarian of the University in whose chapel the Convention was meeting.

These and other men supplemented by a few dollars their inadequate professorial salaries by keeping the college libraries open four or five hours a day, buying the few books the limited appropriations provided for and attending to the necessary administrative chores. Few had other than student assistance; some no help at all. Some of the mechanics' libraries, by the same token, were kept open evenings by young men just starting in business who needed more money to meet living expenses. It is clear that in the majority of American communities libraries did not loom high. The delegates to the 1853 Convention recognized that fact and the very act of getting together for a mutual discussion of their problems showed their keen desire to do something about it.

Chapter Five

ON THE SECOND DAY, FRIDAY THE SIXTEENTH OF SEPTEMBER, Jewett took the floor and held it for nearly the entire morning. After the minutes of the first day's proceedings had been read and approved, and the day's order of business, presented by the Business Committee, had been adopted, and after a few more librarians had made reports, to be added to those received the day before, Samuel F. Haven of the American Antiquarian Society was called to the chair, and Jewett proceeded to give a fairly extended account of the library of the Smithsonian Institution, and followed those remarks by an exposition of its proposed system of cataloging. What he said on that occasion, probably corrected and perhaps amplified, is reported apparently in full in *Norton's Literary and Educational Register, for 1854.*[81] There is little doubt that Jewett's two addresses, or one address in two sections, contained, for the members of that Convention, the most important subject matter to be brought before them, for they had come to look on the Smithsonian Library, under the direction of Charles C. Jewett, as the most powerful influence in bibliothecal circles. Furthermore, they had seen and heard so many reports of Jewett's proposal to make general catalogs with the use of stereotype plates that they were anxious to learn about the proposed process direct from the initiator himself. The newspapers gave more space to this topic than to any other which came before the Convention, several printing Jewett's speech in full. They realized that if Jewett's already publicized method proved to be practical and workable it would revolutionize the making of library catalogs and other bibliographical publications.

The interest of the delegates is understandable. Jewett was doing his utmost to build up a *national* library at the Smithsonian, and although Joseph Henry, the secretary, opposed the plan, it had received the sanction of the Regents, who had voted that half of the Institution's income should be devoted to that purpose. Furthermore, Congress had given its approval. He went to some length in explaining all this to the Convention, but was obliged to report that matters were not going well in that respect, that in the past year only about a thousand dollars had been spent for the purchase of books, and that in the present year a still smaller amount would be thus devoted. Gradually larger and larger proportions of the fund were being appropriated for purposes other than those of the library. Said Jewett,

It was soon found that there were two prominent parties in the Board [of Regents]—not hostile parties, for there is nothing hostile in such matters, but parties of different views in reference to the objects to be pursued by the Institution. One party was in favor of adhering to the library plan, stamped as it was with the approval of Congress; the other was in favor of expending the income in publications and scientific researches. After considerable discussion it was agreed to divide the income of the Institution permanently between the two great departments: that of collections in literature, science and art, and that of publications and scientific researches.

Jewett expressed the firm belief that "a large central library of reference and research" would be collected at the

Smithsonian, if not by government appropriations, then "by other means." He did not indicate, however, what other means he had in mind—if any. "A great central library," continued Jewett, "is an important national object; as necessary to secure the literary independence of this people, as was the war of the Revolution to secure its political independence." But whatever might be the ultimate fate of the attempt to establish a national library at the Smithsonian, Jewett assured his fellow librarians that the collection and publication of statistics of libraries, the increase and dissemination of bibliographical knowledge, and the development and support of the catalog system had met with cordial Regent approval and support; that whatever might be the policy of the Institution with respect to its own collections, it would do all that its means would allow for the benefit of other libraries.

Jewett emphasized the policy of the Smithsonian, of occupying, as far as possible, untenanted ground, and of not attempting, because of its large fund and position of influence, to dictate to other literary institutions of the country. Whenever it was found that any other society or individual was ready or able to carry out certain plans such plans were immediately relinquished by the Institution. Jewett gave as an example of such cooperation and relinquishment *Norton's Literary Gazette*.

Mr. Norton had formed the plan of publishing the *Gazette* without knowing that a similar project had been recommended by myself for the bibliographical department of the Smithsonian Bulletin. He proposed to give the bibliographical intelligence in connection with advertisements, which he thought would eventually be profitable to him. When he saw what I had written, he came on to Washington, and offered to abandon his plan. But we were glad to find that he was willing to undertake to accomplish the same purpose which we had in view, and gave up the whole to him, offering him such assistance as we could render, and encouraging him to believe that the enterprise would prove a profitable one. I am happy to know that his expectation has been fully justified; and I hope that the prosperity of this useful journal will continually increase.

At the final session of the Convention, on Saturday morning, the 17th of September, Elijah Hayward,[82] Ohio's state librarian, introduced this resolution, which was unanimously adopted:

Resolved, That the thanks of this Convention be presented to the Board of Regents and Officers of the Smithsonian Institution, for their steady and effective efforts for the increase and diffusion of knowledge among men, and particularly for the measures which they have adopted for the encouragement and promotion of the public libraries of our country; and we have great pleasure in looking to that institution as the central establishment of the United States for the furtherance of all such objects.

This looks like one of those diplomatic resolutions, intended to make friends and influence people—the Regents of the Smithsonian and the members of Congress. It had its desired effect so far as the increase and diffusion of knowledge was concerned, because that has long been the keynote of the Institution's policy, but it does not appear to have brought about better appropriations by the Regents for its library; for within the year the break came between Henry and Jewett over this very policy, which resulted, as we have seen, in the latter being forced to resign his position. Strangely—to us—there seemed to be throughout this conflict of ideas no thought that the Library of Congress could appropriately become the *national* library. That concept developed later and the Library's growth in the last fifty years is another story. In those days the Library of Congress was the library of *Congress* and nothing more.

After this presentation of information about the Smithsonian Library, Jewett changed his theme and went on to speak of what he modestly termed the "Smithsonian Catalogue System," but which might with propriety have been named for its promoter. The librarians of the country had heard much of this subject in the preceding two or three years. Jewett, in the course of his remarks, referred to a paper he had read before the American Association for the Advancement of Science in August 1850.[83] Several other addresses by him on that topic are recorded in our professional literature. He had also written and the Smithsonian had published in 1852 (Publication No. 47), a pamphlet entitled, *On the Construction of Catalogues of Libraries and a General Catalogue and Their Publication by Means of Separate Stereotype Titles.* A second and enlarged edition was published in 1853, advance copies of which Jewett appears to have had with him at the Convention.

Jewett's plan in brief, as he described it, was to stereotype separately the titles of books and to preserve the plates in alphabetical order of the title, so that additional titles could readily be inserted in their proper places, and thus make possible a way for the reprinting of the whole catalog. The feasibility of the scheme had been studied and reported on favorably by a commission, appointed by the regents of the Smithsonian, consisting of Edward Everett, Charles Folsom, George Livermore, Joseph G. Cogswell, Samuel F. Haven and Edward Everett Hale.

It was thought necessary to find a material cheaper than metal, and, after experimentation, that used was an Indiana clay and shellac, called to his attention, Jewett said, by Josiah Warren,[84] of Indiana. Congress, at Jewett's solicitation, had made an appropriation of $3000 to print, by this method, a section of the catalog of the Library of Congress, as an experiment and demonstration. All of Jewett's colleagues knew well the impossibility of keeping up to date a printed catalog of a growing library by any device then in use, and they were keenly interested in what he, with conviction and enthusiasm, proposed as a remedy for this deficiency. His remarks showed that he had devoted much time, thought and effort toward the working out of his scheme, and, to the majority of his hearers, the process seemed practical.

A basic flaw, however, prevented success. The clay, which appeared to be satisfactory in the experiments and use made of it up to that time, and which would, it was believed, resist longer the wear of the press than type metal, proved not to be a workable medium. It warped and buckled and was entirely unsuitable. It was the old story—the all-important base was lacking. Perhaps Leonardo da Vinci's flying machine might have flown if it had had a gasoline engine!

William F. Poole, recalling incidents in the 1853 Convention in his presidential address before the American Library Association at Milwaukee in 1886 said of the catalog scheme, "I recollect that the librarians of the country generally favored it, and that I did not. I remember that I spoke of it at the time as 'Prof. Jewett's *mud* catalogue' . . . it failed . . . from mechanical defects in the process—the shrinking and warping of the blocks in baking, and the intractable nature of the material when baked, which made the exact adjustment of the blocks on the press impossible."[85]

An important feature of Jewett's plan was for every

library intending to publish catalogs of its books to prepare titles in accordance with rules set forth, and send those titles to the Smithsonian Library, where they would be stereotyped. From those stereotype plates a general catalog of all the books in the country would be compiled. Jewett's keen mind saw the bibliographical need and his active brain worked out a plan which might have succeeded save for the impractical nature of the medium employed.

As Dr. Poole said in his Milwaukee address, the librarians generally favored Jewett's plan. This attitude was expressed in three resolutions presented by Folsom at the conclusion of Jewett's remarks. After a few minor amendments, the purpose of which was to stamp the scheme as purely American and the product of Jewett's brain, the Convention unanimously adopted them at its afternoon session of that second day.

Resolved, That we have considered attentively the plan for constructing catalogues of libraries, and a general catalogue of the public libraries of the United States, by means of separate stereotype titles, originated and proposed by Prof. C. C. Jewett, and developed by him while librarian of the Smithsonian Institution. That we regard it as an object of high importance to the interests of our public libraries, and to the promotion of learning, and worthy to share in the funds of the Institution, and the zealous exertions of its officers; the more so as it is an enterprise which cannot be successfully prosecuted except under the protection, guidance and pecuniary support of this central establishment, for the increase and diffusion of knowledge.

Resolved, That we have learned with pleasure that Congress, on the recommendation of the Library Committee, made an appropriation for the practical testing of the plan in its application to the Library of Congress, and that the work is now in successful progress.

Resolved, That, as practical librarians and bibliographers, we take pride and satisfaction in the fact that a measure of so great literary utility has received the prompt and efficient support of our national legislature, and we would express the earnest hope that this support be extended to it liberally till its first great result, in the complete stereotyped catalogue of the Library of Congress shall be attained.

In the course of the discussion of these resolutions Jewett said that within the past few months he had heard that a claim for this invention had been set up in France, by the Chevalier de Lagarde,[86] an employee of the National Library, who had published a letter in the *Moniteur,* in which he stated that he had formed a similar plan eighteen years previous, that he had published an account of it in 1845, and that he had endeavored to secure its adoption. Jewett said the plan differed in many respects from his own, but still contained the idea of separate stereotype titles. He stated that this claim was entirely unknown to him until long after he had proposed and matured his own system. He expressed the hope that full justice would be done to any earlier efforts.

Samuel F. Haven remarked that in every great discovery there was always found a number of men who claimed to be the originators, but it was universally admitted that he who carried a discovery to its successful application was the one entitled to the credit as inventor.

Charles Folsom said the same idea had struck him thirty years ago, and therefore he had a better claim than the French gentleman, but neither claim amounted to anything, because the idea had produced nothing practical and useful.

Later in that session, Frederic Vinton, of St. Louis, presented the following resolution, the evident object of which was to clear up uncertainties as to the justice of prior claims made in this field.

Resolved, That a Committee of three be appointed by this Convention, to prepare a history of the invention of applying movable stereotype plates to the printing of the separate titles in a catalogue; and that their report be embodied in a written memorial, to be presented at the next annual session of this Convention, in order that it may be printed at the expense of the Convention.

The resolution was unanimously adopted, and Folsom, Guild and Hale were appointed as the committee. The proposer of the resolution, for some unknown reason, was not made a member of it.

Frederic Vinton, Boston born and Amherst educated, was at that time engaged in cataloging the large private library of his brother, in St. Louis, and so registered as from that city. After service in the Boston Public Library and as first assistant librarian of Congress he became the first full-time librarian of the College of New Jersey (Princeton), serving capably in that post from 1873 until his death in 1890.[87] He was one of the few delegates to the 1853 Convention to become a charter member of the American Library Association.[88]

Although Jewett's endeavor, which was, as Dr. Poole said in 1886, "one of the chief topics considered at the Convention," ended in failure and disappointment, it constitutes a notable milestone in the history of catalogs and cataloging, and as such is of interest to us as a serious attempt made nearly a hundred years ago, to solve a vexing problem which, thanks to Halsey W. Wilson,[89] and other pioneers in bibliographical typography, has been solved, in part at least, for our generation.[90]

Chapter Six

PASSING ON TO OTHER MATTERS THAT FRIDAY AFTERNOON, after Jewett's "Catalogue System" had received the consideration they deemed it deserved, the Convention heard Guild, of Brown University, read an extract from a letter written, he said, by the late William Libri, eminent European bibliographer, and addressed to the chairman of the select committee on Public Libraries, which met in London in 1849.[91]

Nothing was more difficult, Libri wrote, than to arrange in the most useful manner the catalog of a large collection of books.

Without speaking of the extremely minute bibliographical researches to which it is necessary to have recourse correctly to describe old works and rare books, the necessity of pointing out . . . all the important facts . . . which may assist the researches of erudite and studious men, creates an enormous labor . . . in which incidental and unexpected questions present themselves, and follow each other with such rapidity as to astonish all men . . . who have not made a special and practical study of this subject. The public, which does not appreciate all these difficulties, is astonished, and gets impatient at delays of which it is ignorant of the causes; but competent men, men who have had experience in the compilation of catalogues, know that they must resign themselves to support that impatience, and to persevere in the

74

path which they have entered, under pain of soon seeing that public which has forced you to hasten your labors, complain of the imperfections it may contain.

Evidently there were both advocates and opponents of simplified and full cataloging even a hundred years ago.

At the first session of the Convention, on Thursday morning, Charles B. Norton "gave notice" that "at a future hour" he would present to the Convention some communications entrusted to him, which were from Vattemare,[92] of Paris, Pertz,[93] of Berlin, and Merlin,[94] of Paris. There is no further mention in the Proceedings of any word from Pertz, but the "communications" from the other two gentlemen were presented by Norton following the letter from Libri, read by Guild. Both papers were fairly long and we doubt that they were read to the delegates. *Norton's Literary Gazette* merely states that the thanks of the Convention were presented to these gentlemen for their communications which were referred to the Business Committee for further consideration. They are printed, apparently in full, in the Proceedings as recorded in the *Register*.[95]

The letter from Romain Merlin (1793-1876), dated Paris, August 29th, 1853, dealt with his system of classification and arrangement of books; and in that era, pre-Cutter, pre-D.C. and pre-L.C., when every library had to devise for itself some arrangement for its books, a proposed system of classification, universally applicable, doubtless was of considerable interest to the librarians of the larger and more scholarly collections. Merlin said that he had long been impressed with the insufficiency of the different classifications in use or proposed, and that he had made this important question the object of his study; that he had in press a work in which, after having reviewed all that had been done up to the present time, he had proposed a new method; and in this letter he proceeded to give its principal points. He said that he had already used this system in several catalogs, including that of the library of the Orientalist, Sylvestre de Sacy, edited by him, in three volumes, Paris, 1843-47, and that in the preface of that work he had shown and explained the application of his system.

Merlin stated that, in his opinion, every systematic arrangement should be based on the logical classification of the sciences, and he had, therefore, sought, in the first place, for the most natural ordering of the different branches of human knowledge, independently of all application to bibliography, and that it was from that order that he had deduced his system.

A system of bibliographical classification, he said, is a logical chain of great classes and their subdivisions, the formation and order of which are the result of a few principles which serve as a base. The object of classification is to assist the memory, by presenting information which will aid the inquirer in his search after books that he already knows exist and give him information about those with which he is unacquainted. This, said he, is almost the same as presenting the literary history of each science in a synoptical form, and the result could be attained only by bringing together all the works that treat on the same subject, and by arranging them in such order that the mind passes naturally from each subject to that which should follow or precede it.

In order that this logical connection should really assist the memory it must be easy to comprehend, and, therefore, if principles are adopted from merely abstract considerations the classification would not accomplish its end; it would be intelligible only to the minds of the few and the best memory would fail to retain it. If, on the contrary, the divisions are taken from the nature of the objects to be classified, and their order is based on the great laws of nature, the system will become intelligible to all, and everyone's memory will be assisted.

In the universality of beings we see, wrote Merlin, as a first division on one side the Creator, on the other the Creation. All ideas which relate to God would form a principal group, which should be designated *Theological Sciences,* and the sciences and arts which treat of created things would be comprised under the common title of *Cosmological Sciences.* Since, however, cause is before effect, the science which treats of God should be before all other sciences. Now Theology, said the French scholar, has only God for its object, and there is another science, namely Philosophy, which treats of God and the Creation; Philosophy, as known to the ancients, treating of first causes, of the essence of being, and of the Creator and created things. Philosophy, therefore, would precede Theology, and after it will come the sciences which relate to created things.

Three great divisions, therefore, spring from this order, noted Merlin: I. Philosophy, II. Theological Sciences, III. Cosmological Sciences. Under the latter he grouped in order, mathematics, physics, astronomy, geology, mineralogy, botany, zoology, and anthropology. Man should be considered under two heads, individual man and man in society. Individual man resolved itself into two divisions, physical man and moral man. Man in society also furnished two divisions, the social or political sciences and the historical sciences.

Merlin closed his communication by saying that he should

be much honored if his method were judged worthy of being applied to the literary collections being made in America, and one readily recognizes that the principal classifications now in use in American libraries have much in common with the system proposed by this learned French bibliographer nearly one hundred years ago.

The second "communication" laid by Norton before the Convention was from Alexandre Vattemare, dated Paris, August 22, 1853, and it dealt with the writer's pet hobby, international exchanges.

Vattemare was well known to that body of men, as his efforts to establish and operate international exchanges of books and museum specimens between European and American institutions had doubtless been brought to the attention of nearly every library there represented. He was, by profession, a ventriloquist and actor, and had appeared, with marked success, at most of the courts and before most of the crowned heads of Europe. Born in Paris near the end of the eighteenth century, he spent much of his time, energy, and property from about 1827 until his death in 1864 enthusiastically promoting his schemes for international exchanges—more time and energy, in fact, than he devoted to his art. In going about Europe in his professional capacity in the 1820's and '30's this predecessor of Edgar Bergen had been impressed with the great numbers of duplicates lying idle and useless in nearly every library, private or public, which he visited, and he was seized with the determination, entered into with all his Gallic impetuosity, to put these idle books to work by placing them, through the medium of exchange, in libraries which lacked them. In 1839 he made his first visit to America expressly on this mission and came again in 1847 and for a third time in 1848. His spar-

kling personality and rosy promises to cure the woeful lack
of reference books in the libraries of the new world had gal-
vanized ordinarily phlegmatic members of Congress and of
state and city governments into action with the result that
what were then looked on as liberal appropriations were
made from federal, state and city funds to put the machinery
of his exchange scheme into operation.

Vattemare's extraordinary eloquence and enthusiasm had
been strongly felt on both sides of the Atlantic and it is not
strange that he was quick to grasp the opportunity to present
his plan and make a report on its progress to the convened
librarians. In his *Memorial History of Boston*,[96] Justin
Winsor wrote,

Whatever we may think of Vattemare, whether we call him an
enthusiast, or something worse or better, we must recognize his
contagious energy, which induced state after state to succumb
to his representations, so that by 1853 he had brought one hundred and thirty libraries and institutions within his operations,
and between 1847 and 1851 had brought from France for American libraries 30,655 volumes, besides maps, engravings, etc.

By his insistence of Boston's need for a public library
and by a collection of books brought from France, Vattemare was one of the instruments in the establishment of
the Boston Public Library. "To him more than to any
other man," wrote Josiah P. Quincy, in 1885,[97] "we owe the
foundations of the great public library which is the pride
of this city."

The respect shown to Vattemare by the Convention is
evidenced by the fact that eight of the forty-six pages devoted to the Proceedings of the Convention in *Norton's
Literary and Educational Register, for 1854*,[98] are given to
his letter and its accompanying tables.

"The whole of my system is there," said he, of these tables, taking apparent pride that they had been "submitted some months ago to the Emperor, and prepared by order of his majesty." The first table gives a list of one hundred twenty-five libraries, government departments, cities, colleges and other establishments in Europe and America which "have participated in the benefits of the system of exchanges." Of these, seventy-four were in the United States, and included "All the Departments of the Federal Government" (listed as one entry), "The Presidential Residence," "Library of Congress," and most of the then active colleges, state, and city historical societies and nineteen of the principal cities of the country.

The second table was a chronological list of the official acts and documents by which the several governments on both sides of the ocean had accepted the principle or "regulated the application of the system of exchange," from 1832 to 1853.

Seventeen States of the Union, reported Vattemare, had adopted similar laws to that of Congress, referring to the granting of a federal appropriation, on June 30, 1848, to help promote the system. And in conclusion he recorded that from 1847 to 1851 inclusive, 61,011 books and pamphlets had been placed by his exchange system, of which 30,655, as reported by Justin Winsor, went to American institutions. To Norton Vattemare wrote,

As for the system, it is gaining ground rapidly in Europe. By a letter dated St. Petersburg, 29th July last, received the day I had the pleasure of seeing you, His Excellency the Baron de Korff, Counsellor of State, and Director of the Imperial Library of St. Petersburg, acknowledging the receipt of the Natural History of the State of New York, informs me that, after mature consideration, convinced of the important services our system of exchange is likely to render, he sends me the list of a series of most valuable duplicates of incunabula in the Imperial Library, to be placed at my disposal. The Danish Government has also presented, through its minister here, a list of splendid ancient works. The librarians of some of the celebrated Universities of Germany have made similar communications. . . .

You have seen the fine series of ancient and modern books they were selecting for me at the Imperial Library. The little time you spent in my office was yet sufficient to give you an idea of what may be obtained from our system. You saw all the nations side by side, republicans and imperialists holding each other by the hand to help the realization of our great and peaceful Republic of Letters.

Let me close this letter by expressing my grateful acknowledgment towards the States and institutions of the Union, that have so readily and so nobly given a helping hand to my efforts, and tell them that, in my conviction, the time is not distant when they will reap the advantages of that generous and persevering support; that the little that has been done is only the earnest of what is yet to come. . . .

. . . Have the kindness to say to these learned gentlemen, how happy I would have been to have found myself among so many distinguished savants, many of whom have shown themselves so benevolent to me, and in a country whose generous and fraternal hospitality I shall never forget.

Vattemare's ambitious scheme did not materialize to the extent envisioned by its magnetic initiator. It lacked organization and so with its author's death in 1864 it passed into the realm of worthy things uncompleted. But the ever-present interest in the principle of exchanges, especially of international exchanges, gives today's librarians an added feeling of kinship to their professional forbears of 1853.

The "communications" of the French gentlemen having been received and appropriately dealt with, the Convention passed on to other matters.

Complying, we fancy, with the request that the delegates come prepared to make some contribution to the program, Lloyd P. Smith, of the Philadelphia Library, presented a paper on the classified index he was compiling, which simplified greatly the task of making sure whether or not a certain book was "in." We surmise that Smith's paper was not read at the Convention, because the *Gazette,* which, as we have said, gave a nearly chronological order to the various items of business, makes no reference to it, and the *Register* placed it between the communication from Merlin and that from Vattemare.[99]

The day of open shelves had not arrived—at least not in the Philadelphia Library—nor had that of systematic classification, as we are reminded by the primitive "fixed" location of books reported on as obtaining in that already venerable institution.

Smith said that the Philadelphia Library had been in existence one hundred and twenty-one years and possessed 65,000 volumes. The books were arranged on the shelves "according to a plan perhaps somewhat peculiar; that is, simply according to size." There were four sets of numbers, viz., folios, quartos, octavos, and duodecimos. The plan, he said, had some advantages as well as some disadvantages. It gave a neat and uniform appearance to the books as they stood on the shelves, and it made it easy to ascertain whether or not a book was "in." It had the disadvantage, he admitted, that the works on the same subject were not together. This was, however, less important with them than in those libraries where the cases were open to the public.

Their books were always kept under lock and key, the titles on the books being visible through the wires which protected them. When a book was wanted the catalog indicated the number and size. It was obvious, he said, that in their system this dependence on the catalog made a good one of the greatest importance.

Smith then went on to describe their general printed catalog, its two supplements and the inconvenience of looking for a book without some such aid as his classified index would provide. As one reads what to this generation of librarians seems such primitive and obvious directions for the making of so fundamental a tool, and Smith's methods of shelving books, so long since discarded, one realizes that in some respects at least library technique and practice have made progress in the last hundred years.

At that point in the second day's business Charles Folsom exhibited a plan of his own for arranging catalog entries conveniently for printing. His scheme has a familiar ring and it dawns on us that inventive and forward-looking souls, like the librarian of the Boston Athenaeum, were in 1853 discovering the principles of the card catalog.

Folsom reported, according to the secretary's account in the *Gazette*[100] (the *Register* omits this feature), that his plan

consisted of a series of cards, about nine inches long and two wide, which were laid in a pile, and a hole bored through each end of the whole, and strings passed through them. These strings were of such a length as to allow the whole of the cards to be slid back or forward, as the writer or compositor should find necessary, yet still preserving them in their proper order, without confusion or danger of loss. The whole were fitted into a box of the requisite size, from which they could be drawn singly, without deranging the consecutiveness of each.

As the thanks of the Convention were given to Folsom for describing this and other ingenious devices, such as a steel clasp for keeping large folios in a compact state, and a table on which a book of any size could be kept at the desired angle, Samuel F. Haven remarked that they had long known the talents of Mr. Folsom in matters of literature and science, but now they had proof of his mechanical genius as well.[101]

At this point in the proceedings Reuben Guild presented the following resolutions relative to their next meeting and the formation of a permanent organization:

Resolved, That this Convention be regarded as preliminary to the formation of a permanent Librarians' Association.

Resolved, That a Committee of five be appointed to draft a Constitution and By-Laws for such an Association, and present them at the next meeting of the Convention.

Resolved, That when this Convention adjourn, it adjourn to meet in Washington City at such a time as the said Committee of five may appoint.

Resolved, That this Committee be requested, with reference to this adjourned meeting, to suggest topics for written communications or free discussion, and also to make such other arrangements as shall, in their judgment, be best adapted to meet the needs of the public, in regard to the whole subject of Libraries and library economy.

In accordance with these resolutions, which were unanimously adopted, the Committee for Permanent Organization was appointed as follows: C. C. Jewett, Charles Folsom, S. Hastings Grant, Elijah Hayward, and R. A. Guild.

Before they adjourned on that busy second day, Guild, the champion "resolver," moved that the official report of the proceedings be furnished to the editor of *Norton's Literary Gazette* with the request that they be published in the next

(October 15) number. Unanimously voted, and, as we have seen, the Proceedings were so published, and also in a fuller and more carefully edited form in *Norton's Literary and Educational Register, for 1854*, which came out in December of 1853.

Guild next moved that grateful acknowledgments be tendered to the chancellor and faculty of the University in whose building on Washington Square they were meeting for their kindness in granting free use of their chapel and rooms during the sessions of the Convention, and also "to the gentlemen of this City who have so generously provided for our comfort and entertainment." These resolutions were, of course, unanimously carried.

The chancellor to whom these acknowledgments were made was the fifty-five-year-old Dutch Reformed clergyman, Isaac Ferris, who, in the previous year, after several successful pastorates, had left the pulpit of the Market Street Church in New York to direct the destinies of the debt-involved University of the City of New York, which had been acephalous for the preceding two years and was rapidly drifting toward chaos. He was a good executive and "his majestic presence, confident address, and wholesome courage," to quote his biographer, "inspired confidence." In short order he not only got the institution out of debt but added materially to its funds and raised the standards of scholarship. His name is on the roll as one who attended the Librarians' Convention, but whether he merely looked in and signed the register or whether he actually participated in the deliberations it is now impossible to say.

And so, "on motion, the Convention adjourned to 9 o'clock Saturday morning," and we know from newspaper references, though not from the Proceedings, that the delegates then accepted Dr. Cogswell's invitation and went over to inspect the new Astor Library, which would shortly open its doors to the public. And that evening, as we have seen, the delegates from "abroad" (out of town, to us) were entertained by their New York colleagues with an 8 o'clock repast and reception at the Kemble House around on 19th Street.

Chapter Seven

ON SATURDAY, SEPTEMBER 17, THE THIRD AND LAST DAY, PRESI-
dent Jewett called the Convention to order soon after nine
o'clock. Secretary Grant was "temporarily absent" and
Daniel C. Gilman was requested to act as secretary *pro tem.*
Reading of the minutes was dispensed with. Perhaps the
absent Grant had them in his pocket! Aside from the inclusion of his name in the list of delegates and the statement
by Yale's absent librarian that if any assessments were levied
his friend, Daniel Gilman, would pay them on his behalf,
this is the only reference in the Proceedings to the future
president of Johns Hopkins University; but we have seen
how active young Gilman was in helping to make arrangements for the Convention, and we have already ventured the
surmise that, so far as time permitted before he sailed for
Europe, he helped Hastings Grant in the preparation of the
Proceedings.

After a few announcements were made and the order of
business for the day had been reported by Chairman Folsom
of the Business Committee and resolutions, already here reported, on a couple of subjects had been acted on, John
William Wallace, Librarian of the Philadelphia Law Association, addressed the chair and offered the following resolutions, "which he introduced with a few appropriate
remarks."

87

Resolved, As a sense of this Convention, that the completeness of public law libraries throughout the country, and the interest of American jurisprudence, would be promoted by having, in each incorporated or public law library of the United States, a complete set of the *Statutes at large* of every State of the Union, in their original and unabridged condition. And that, as these volumes appear only from year to year, as they are not often on sale by law booksellers, nor easily procured from year to year by application, therefore, that this Convention respectfully suggests to the Governors, Secretaries of State, Legislatures or other public authorities having power to distribute these volumes, to make some permanent orders for transmitting to the Smithsonian Institution, at Washington, for distribution to the library of the Law Association at Philadelphia, and to the other public or incorporated law libraries throughout the United States, a certain number of copies of their statute laws, as published from year to year by the Legislatures of the respective States, in the original and unabridged condition.

Resolved, That the Secretary of the Law Association of Philadelphia, be requested, with leave of that body, to transmit a copy of this resolution to the respective Governors and Secretaries of State throughout the Union, with any remarks he may see proper to make on the subject.

Whatever favorable effect these commendable resolutions, which were unanimously passed, may have had on the practice of "Governors, Secretaries of State, Legislatures or other public authorities" in supplying their respective statutes at large to the various law libraries we do not know, but the resolutions are interesting as further indication of the growing desire to have the Smithsonian Institution serve the country as a distributing agency for publications given or exchanged. American and foreign libraries have a deep sense of gratitude for the cheerful way in which this irksome function has been performed for nearly a hundred years by this official Washington agency.

Reuben Guild, indisputably the Convention's Number One Resolution Presenter, then offered the following:

Resolved, That the members of this Convention cordially recommend the mutual exchange, so far as may be practicable, of the printed catalogues of all our public libraries.

This resolution, like all others to come before the Convention, was unanimously passed.

Few of the many resolutions adopted were carried out, chiefly because no further conference of librarians was held for nearly a quarter of a century, but we fancy that, as a result of the above, probably a considerable exchange of catalogs was made by various libraries over the country. Perhaps one of the chief benefits of the Convention was that a large number of librarians got to know each other personally, became not only acquainted but concerned with the other man's problems, and so brought in the era of professional co-operation by which we have all profited.

The next action taken was the approval of a plan for an index of American newspapers and "chronology of important events for the last 125 years." The author of the plan was Edwin Williams, a member of the library committee of the American Institute, but, as he was presumably not present that Saturday morning, it was presented on his behalf by Samuel F. Haven, of the American Antiquarian Society.

Williams, in a statement signed by him, explained his plan. As a member of the New York Historical Society he said he had brought before one of its meetings a proposal for an index to be made of the principal American newspapers in their files, extending over the last one hundred and twenty-five years. The proposal was, he said, favorably received by the Society and referred to a special committee, of which he was chairman, with power to carry the project into effect. He desired an expression of the opinion of the Convention on the subject, believing that such an index was important to the interests of "Historical Literature, as it must open new sources of information, particularly to those engaged in researches either for literary or business purposes."

The plan, Williams's statement went on to say, proposed an index and chronological arrangement of the most important matters relative to American history, which may be found in the newspapers in the library of the New York Historical Society, principally those published in the city of New York, from about 1728 to that present year, 1853. The index, he said, should include also the volumes of the *National Intelligencer,* which had been published at Washington for the last half century, and might also embrace the volumes of *Niles' Register,* published in Baltimore, from 1811 to 1849.

He estimated that the proposed index would probably comprise two octavo volumes of about one thousand pages, arranged on the plan of Holmes's *American Annals;* that five or more persons could be employed in the work of preparing the index; and that the time required need not exceed two years. The Society would publish the work in an edition of a thousand or fifteen hundred copies at a total estimated expense of ten thousand dollars—one half for the preparation, and one half for printing and binding. To provide for this expense it was proposed to obtain two hundred subscribers at fifty dollars each, each subscriber receiving five copies of the work.[102]

Although this worthy plan was not carried through, and the proposed index was not made and published, it is interesting to know that nearly a hundred years ago the importance of newspapers to historical study was recognized and the need felt for making more accessible the information contained in them.

It is interesting likewise to note that this proposal of a committee of the New York Historical Society and the resolution of the Convention approving it should have been presented by a librarian of the American Antiquarian Society, recalling, as it does, the debt historical scholarship owes to another head of that venerable institution, Clarence S. Brigham, whose work on the bibliography of early American newspapers has been helpful to so many.

Charles Folsom then offered the following resolution, intended obviously to help hold up the hands of Jewett in his endeavor to build up a national library at the Smithsonian.

Resolved, That the establishment of a great central library for reference and research, while it is demanded by the condition of the United States as to general civilization and intellectual advancement, is especially interesting to this Convention from the bearing it would have upon libraries throughout the country.

Resolved, That we deem such an establishment as being eminently worthy of support from the national treasury, and that in no way can the government better promote the progress of learning through the whole country than by placing a central national library under the administration of the Smithsonian Institution.

Although these resolutions were unanimously adopted they had small effect on the policy of that institution.

The Convention's attention was next directed to the need for the establishment of small public libraries in the various towns, villages and schools of the country, and this was done, not by a librarian, but by a school principal, the Reverend Gorham D. Abbott,[103] of the Spingler Institute, of New York, who presented the following resolution:

Resolved, That the time has now arrived when the extension of well-selected public libraries, of 1,000, 5,000 and 10,000 volumes, throughout the towns and villages, the associations, the institutions, the schools of every kind in the United States, has become a matter of the greatest importance to the future welfare of our country.

Resolved, That a committee of three be appointed to report a digested plan for the promotion of this object at the next meeting of this Convention.

Edward Everett Hale seconded the resolutions and in a speech of some length expressed the hope that some means might be found to carry out the principle. But he called attention to the danger which, he considered, lurked in every such plan, namely, to compile selected lists of books: that as soon as such a list was suggested, there started up a bookseller's job, and the benefit of the list was lost in the struggles of those who sought to be the only publishers who could supply the libraries. The school boards of the various states, he said, had found this difficulty so incurable that they had refrained from suggesting any list of school books as an official list to be followed.

Hale then took the opportunity to attempt some definition of a "popular" library, words which had, he reminded his hearers, been frequently used in the sessions of the Convention. There were, he said, two distinct meanings of the word "popular," one referred to something at the moment

92

attractive, as the playing of Miss Julia Dean,[104] the "popular" actress. There was also "popular" in the sense of "real use to the whole people," and in that sense only does the resolution contemplate a popular library.

The great duty and the great difficulty, continued Hale, of the trustees of popular libraries is to keep them true to this sort of popularity, and to turn as sternly as possible from the temptation to buy books which are popular, only because at the moment attractive, for this class of purchases becomes the most costly possible. In a few years, or even in a few months, such books lose all their attraction, and the library which has bought them at the highest price and has had to give them shelf room afterwards finds they are worth really nothing at all.

That "magnificent enterprise" which had made books cheaper in America than in any country of the world made it easy for every man to get hold of the cheap literature which is simply transitory in character, so that there was no need to accumulate that in a public library. "The youngster who had bought for a shilling," said Hale, "the fascinating account of the Russian campaign, by Alexander Dumas, has a right to find in the public library the more fascinating pages of the Count Segur, from which it is drawn."

All of this has a familiar sound, for we realize that Edward Everett Hale was touching on the same book policies which have been discussed and debated by library trustees and librarians ever since his time. All of us, we fear, have not yet caught up with the book-acquisition views set forth by this broad-minded preacher and writer nearly a century ago.

The resolutions to which Hale was speaking were, of

course, adopted, and Messrs. Haven,[105] Abbott and Jewett were named as the committee to report at the "next annual meeting."

The first edition of Poole's *Index to Periodicals* had just been published by Charles B. Norton and a copy of that now rare book had evidently been circulating among the delegates. On motion, therefore, of Charles Folsom, Poole's Boston neighbor, it was unanimously

> *Resolved,* That we have examined the work entitled "Index to Periodicals," by W. F. Poole, Librarian of the Mercantile Library of Boston, and that we approve of the plan and execution, and we recommend that a similar system of indexing be extended to the transactions and memoirs of learned societies.

This is the only reference in the Proceedings to the man who later was to become the most prominent librarian who attended that 1853 Convention. His silence would not appear to have been due to youthfulness, because he was only four or five years younger than the president of that body. And the interest he took in the negotiations is unmistakably reflected in the recollections he gave in his address as president of the American Library Association at Milwaukee in 1886. We surmise that Poole was by no means silent during those three days but that he preferred to engage in informal conversation and discussion between sessions rather than to raise his voice on the floor of the house.

Mr. Folsom next read a paper which had been written by him on the Boston Athenaeum and the duties and qualifications of librarians. A request was made that he permit the paper to be published, but he said it had been written as a letter to a friend and he considered it the property of the one to whom it was originally addressed and therefore that he could not, with propriety, give it to the public. Speaking of the letter, the *New York Tribune* of September 19th said: "The venerable librarian seemed thoroughly inspired with the subject. The article read was redolent of the glorious spirit of the authors whose society he had so long cultivated, and was much applauded."

The letter Folsom read on this occasion was addressed by him to Samuel Atkins Eliot, treasurer of Harvard College, and father of Charles W. Eliot, and was dated TEMPLE PLACE, 27th October, 1845. It was printed in the *Proceedings* of the Massachusetts Historical Society for April, 1873 (p. 28-34), as a part of the "Memoir of Charles Folsom," by Theophilus Parsons. The latter states that a few copies were printed for private circulation, but that it had never been published. "It is full of good sense," says Parsons, "gives the results of his own experience and observation, and in delineating the character of a consummate librarian he unintentionally draws a portrait of himself."

This is how Folsom regarded the duty of a librarian, as set forth by him in his letter to Samuel Eliot.

Its [the library's] treasures should be *guarded* from age to age with scrupulous care. The beauty of order should pervade their arrangement. The books should be kept in perfect condition as to their binding; and the appropriate binding and lettering of books often involve knowledge and taste enough to bring them within the outer circle of the fine arts. The custodian should have a *respect* for books, and seek, by his example, to inspire others with it. Books in the shops are manufactures, merchandise,—and cost so much. In a fair library, good books are shrines, oracles,—great minds marshalled in glorious companies, uttering the wisdom of past ages, or of an age that will soon be past.

My temperament is not eminently poetical, and I have had

much to do with the mechanical manufacture of *volumes;* but I honor the man whose mind readily transmutes a goodly *book* into an *author.* I shall never forget the awe, the emotion, akin to the sublime, with which, when declining day had left me in dim twilight in the old library at Cambridge, I have passed along by the alcoves, as if in the immediate presence of the illustrious dead; and when, on some rare occasion, I have gone alone, late in the evening, to seek a book, with no light but the halo around saints and sages, the feeling has been almost overpowering. Had I been one whom we wot of, you would long since have heard another solemn and tender "Voice of the night."

All this means only, that a library is a *sanctum;* and whatever relates to the *keeping* of the books, and the preservation of due quiet, should be *the subject of precise rules,* which, in *the most courteous spirit,* should be enforced when necessary; and any odium arising therefrom in the minds of unreasonable people should be assumed by the Trustees, to whom the Librarian is immediately responsible.

The duties of a Librarian as the *dispenser* of a great Library. The office of *custodian* has, so far as I know, always been satisfactorily performed at the Athenaeum. Not so, I believe, the other branch of a Librarian's duty. By *dispensing,* I am far from meaning only the finding of the particular volumes asked for, or the recording of the titles of such as are borrowed. I mean quite another ability in the Librarian,—an ability to "bring forth, out of the treasure" committed to him, "things new and old." He should be passably skilled in ancient and modern languages; should be acquainted with the history of literature; should know the external history of books, and have some notion of their contents, understanding at least their scope and bearing, so as to be able readily to follow out subjects, and to put inquirers upon the right track. To many, the very multitude of books is confusing, and days of research are lost in a wrong direction, which a few words from an intelligent Librarian might at once prevent. . . .

96

Charles Folsom was born in Exeter, New Hampshire, in 1794 and he died in 1872. Admiral Farragut, when a youth, was one of Folsom's pupils and was his lifelong friend and admirer. He was the Boston Athenaeum's librarian from 1845 to 1856, and on his retirement the trustees of the Athenaeum put on their minutes this resolution:

Resolved, That the Trustees of the Boston Athenaeum have received with sincere regret the resignation of Mr. Charles Folsom as Librarian,—an office which he has held for more than ten years, performing the various and difficult duties of the place with devoted fidelity, and securing thereby the respect and affection not only of the Trustees, but also of numerous proprietors and visitors of the Athenaeum.

Following Folsom's paper a vote of thanks was passed to the American Geographical and Statistical Society and to the New York Historical Society "for the freedom of their rooms and other facilities afforded by them." As these societies had their quarters in the building of the University, in the chapel of which the Convention was held, it is probable that the librarians were given the use of their rooms for committee meetings and informal gatherings between sessions.

George H. Moore, the librarian of the Historical Society, in replying, said that circumstances of no ordinary nature had detained him from the earlier sessions and expressed his hearty sympathy with the objects of the Convention.

John Disturnell, a member of the American Geographical and Statistical Society, then read a paper proposing a plan for the preparation of a catalog of works "relating to American history, geography, and statistics of population, emigration, agriculture, internal improvements, minerals, coinage and banking." The historical and geographical works, in-

97

cluding maps and charts, he stated, should date from the discovery of America by Columbus to the present time; statistical works should date from the first census of 1790 to the present period. The era of scholarly scientific bibliography was soon to burst on the world and Disturnell doubtless felt it in the air. Whether any of the later bibliographies of Americana can be traced to his suggestion would be difficult to tell. His paper was referred to the standing committee and that, so far as we know, was as far as it got.

The Convention was now nearing its close and the usual courtesy motions were in order.

Elijah Hayward, state librarian of Ohio, opened by offering a resolution presenting the thanks of the Convention to the president, secretary, and business committee "for the ability, attention, industry, courtesy, and gentlemanly deportment" with which they had discharged their several and respective duties, and resolving that "we now part from them and from each other with feelings of the kindest regard."

Hayward, who was librarian of the Ohio State Library from 1851 to 1854 had been, years before (1825-28), a member of the Ohio house of representatives from Hamilton County (Cincinnati), and his resolution, which was unanimously passed, as such resolutions always are, has the flavor of the tactful legislator.

Then, on motion of George H. Moore, a vote of thanks—and well-deserved thanks—was tendered to Charles B. Norton, "for the earnest and disinterested manner in which he had advanced the interests of this Convention, both at home and abroad." Norton, in a few words, expressed his sense of the honor done him.

And then, recorded Secretary Grant, Professor Jewett congratulated the Convention on the harmony and results of their meeting, which he attributed to the absence of all sinister or selfish aims. They had come there with differences of opinion, indeed, and topics had been freely discussed; yet, he was proud to say, in all their transactions there had been no negative vote. He also expressed appreciation of the manner in which their proceedings had been reported by the press.

By that time it was undoubtedly past noon and time to go. All formal papers had been submitted and acted on; all the addresses, impromptu and otherwise, had been made; all the numerous resolutions had been adopted—unanimously adopted, as Jewett had just reminded them; all items of business had been disposed of. Nothing more remained to be done.

And so, reported Secretary Grant, "the Convention adjourned to meet at Washington, at the call of the . . . committee."

As the delegates passed out of the "smaller chapel," on that September noon in 1853, and left for homes and libraries they would doubtless have been amazed could they have known that the next meeting of librarians would not be held in Washington, "at the call of the committee," but in Philadelphia, twenty-three years later!

Chapter Eight

SO THE LIBRARIAN'S CONVENTION OF 1853, THE FIRST HELD
in this or any country so far as known, passed into history.
That they expected soon to meet again was reiterated by
the librarians time and again in the course of their three
days' business: in the address of President Jewett when he
expressed the hope "that this Convention may be the precursor of a permanent and highly useful association"; in
the resolution of the Reverend Samuel Osgood, regarding
the preparation of a library manual and the appointment of
a committee to report "at the next meeting of the Convention"; in the resolution of Frederic Vinton proposing that a
history of the invention of movable stereotype plates be
presented "at the next meeting of this Convention"; in the
resolution that a committee be appointed to report a plan
for the extension of public libraries "at the next meeting
of this Convention"; and especially in the resolutions on
permanent organization introduced by Guild and unanimously adopted.

But notwithstanding this frequently expressed intention,
no meeting of librarians, as we have said, was again held
until 1876, when the American Library Association was
organized. There were several reasons. Jewett was, as we
have seen, named chairman of this committee of five, whose
duty was to arrange for the next convention, and when he

summarily quit his post as librarian of the Smithsonian Institution and left Washington, the heart was taken out of the movement. Jewett was their big man—their leader—and he was no longer in Washington, where they had voted to meet, and not in his former position of governmental influence. And none of the other members of the committee apparently felt disposed to take the initiative. In four years the great depression of 1857 hit the country and undoubtedly affected libraries and the purses of librarians. Soon after that came the War between the States, to be followed by the bleak and bitter years of reconstruction. All of which brings us down to 1876. There were doubtless other reasons too, but these were enough.

That consideration was given to a meeting in 1854 is shown by a letter from Jewett to Grant on May 11 of that year. Grant had written, it appears, to Jewett on the 9th. This letter has been lost but it apparently touched on plans for the next convention—perhaps that was its main theme, although as the last sentence implies, one purpose may have been to ask for a copy, or copies, of Jewett's rules for cataloging. This is Jewett's letter:

Charles C. Jewett to S. Hastings Grant[106]

WASHINGTON 11 MAY 1854

MY DEAR SIR,

I am happy to acknowledge the receipt of your letter of the 9th inst. I have felt in great doubt what to do or to recommend with respect to our convention. I have been so peculiarly situated that I have not, at any time during the Spring, felt that it would be proper for me to invite our brethren here. I have been every week hoping to see my way clear by *the next week*. Thus have I been beguiled.

The convention adjourned to meet "*in Washington at such*

time as the said Committee may appoint." The place is fixed—
the time is not. Have we the right to change the place? We
might perhaps by consent of all members obtained by sending
circulars to all members. But, would it not be better to meet
here next autumn? Is it not upon the whole better to meet but
once a year and to prepare ourselves well for each meeting? Mr.
Livermore with whom I have conversed thinks best to meet next
September or some time later.

There has been an almost uninterrupted succession of Conventions here, this Spring, National Agricultural, Congregational,
Scientific Association, Superintendents of Hospitals, National
Education, etc., crowding upon each other so fast that no one
created any distinct and decided impression. During the session
of Congress, and particularly while any exciting question is under
discussion, such conventions are but little noticed here. Even
the Scientific Association produced no considerable impression.
Scarcely a dozen citizens of Washington were present at any
meeting. I think not half a dozen members of Congress during
all the meetings. The citizens of Washington subscribed liberally and entertained handsomely—but their hospitality has been
severely taxed this Spring. There is no one in the city particularly
interested in our objects except Col. Force. Mr. Riggs will be
here next autumn and then I can probably interest Mr. Corcoran
and others.

I hope to see you in New York next week or the week after
and talk over these matters with you. We will then consider more
fully what announcement had better be made.

I have no copies of the Rules for cataloguing but expect to
have some soon—and will then send as you request.

I remain

Very sincerely yours,

C. C. JEWETT

S. H. Grant, Esq.

The peculiar situation referred to was without doubt the

strained relations between Joseph Henry and Jewett over the library policy, which led, as we have already stated, to the latter's sudden termination of his Smithsonian librarianship in the summer of 1854, so that by autumn, which Jewett thought an appropriate time to meet, he was no longer in Washington.

In view of the willingness of committees in more recent times to accept responsibilities for the readjustments of situations to meet changed conditions it seems strange that the Permanent Committee of five did not—at least Jewett, the chairman, did not—feel disposed to cut the Gordian knot and, the Convention's resolution notwithstanding, meet somewhere else than in Washington, if it seemed necessary or desirable to make a change of place. But their inflexible notion appears to have been one of the reasons why no successor to the 1853 Convention was held.

Reuben Guild in 1899 wrote a letter of Convention reminiscences for the Unitarian Club of Providence. This was read at the Magnolia (1902) Conference of the American Library Association[107] by Charles W. Jencks, to whom the letter was addressed.

You ask me about the great Librarians' Convention, that was held in New York, Sept. 15 and 17, 1853, which you attended as librarian of Mechanics' Library, Providence, and which I attended as librarian of Brown University. That was forty-six years ago, when we were young men. In looking over the twenty-one names that signed the call for the meeting I recognized, as among the living, beside myself, Rev. Edward Everett Hale, Hon. Henry Barnard, and S. Hastings Grant. My recollections of the Convention are very distinct. It was the first convention of the kind ever held in the world's history.

. . . The Convention adjourned to meet in Washington, after

appointing a committee of five to arrange for permanent organization. The committee failed to make arrangements, and there was no further meeting of the librarians until 1876, when the present American Library Association was organized in Philadelphia. The Committee on permanent organization has been criticised for its failure to act. The chairman, Professor Jewett, about this time had a controversy with Dr. Henry of the Smithsonian Institution, and eventually left Washington to organize the Public Library of Boston. He was too busy to arrange for another convention. The second man on the committee, Prof. Charles Folsom, resigned as librarian of the Boston Athenaeum, and no longer served the cause. The third, S. Hastings Grant, gave up his position as librarian of the Mercantile Library and went into politics on a much larger salary. Elijah Hayward, the fourth, lived in Ohio, and the fifth man, your humble servant, did not feel inclined to shoulder the burden alone. Besides, the prime mover in the first Convention, Gen. Charles B. Norton, had met with reverses and was unable to go on as in the beginning, acting as an agent of librarians. Then came the financial crisis of 1857, the Civil War, reconstruction, etc. The tenth meeting of the American Library Association was held at the Thousand Islands, so called, in 1887. This meeting you and I attended.

Dr. Guild's memory at seventy-seven and within a few weeks of his death was at fault in a few particulars. The Boston Public Library was well along in its organization before Jewett went there. Folsom did not retire until 1856, and Grant held his post at the New York Mercantile Library until 1866. And, to be meticulous, twenty-six and not twenty-one names were signed to the call.

Fifteen members of the 1853 Convention lived to become either active or honorary members of the American Library Association, the "permanent organization" they themselves hoped to form. Two of this number, William Frederick

Poole and Frederic Vinton were charter members. In 1902 the American Library Association elected to honorary membership all known survivors of the 1853 meeting. They were these eight: Willard Fiske, Daniel Coit Gilman, S. Hastings Grant, Edwin H. Grant, the Rev. Edw. E. Hale, Ezekiel A. Harris, Chas. W. Jencks, and Dr. Anson Judd Upson. News of the death of Professor Upson on June 15 came while the Conference was in session.

The last survivor, so far as I have knowledge, was Ezekiel A. Harris, who was librarian of the American Institute in 1853. I had the pleasure of calling upon him in March 1916, at his home in Jersey City, and found him in vigorous health of mind and body notwithstanding his eighty-five years.[108] To my disappointment he was unable to throw additional light on the conduct of the Convention, for as a youth of twenty-two he did not realize, he said, the professional historic nature of the gathering and took no active part in it. He remembered the energetic aggressive personality of Charles B. Norton and the genial courtesy of Grant; Jewett was looked up to and lionized by all present; Folsom was respected as their *Nestor;* Lloyd Smith was regarded as an exceptional scholar and "coming man." Of others than these he had no recollections. His impressions of Poole, Gilman and Hale dated from a later period. Edwin Williams, as a member of the library committee, was the official delegate from the American Institute, and Ezekiel Harris, its librarian, confessed that he was, at the time, more concerned with finishing at an early date a catalog of the library on which he was then working, and a printed copy of which he still had on his desk after all the intervening years, than in attending the sessions of a convention.

Harris said he served as librarian of the American Institute until 1859, when he went to Tennessee to engage in business, but returned north two years later at the outbreak of the War. For many years he was in commercial work in New York, but for the twenty years previous to 1916 had been actively occupied with religious and charitable work in Jersey City. He expressed deep appreciation at being elected to honorary membership in the A.L.A., but modestly felt that his part in the 1853 Convention was not significant enough to entitle him to such recognition.

In 1887 the American Library Association held its annual Conference at the Thousand Islands, and Charles B. Norton, remembering the old days and the first Convention of librarians, attempted to gather some of his 1853 colleagues at this meeting of the A.L.A., chiefly, we suspect, for reminiscence. The "get-together" effort was only partly successful,[109] but the preserved correspondence is interesting.

S. Hastings Grant to Charles B. Norton[110]

PIERMONT, N.Y., AUG. 29, 1887

MY DEAR MR. NORTON:

Your esteemed note of the 26th inst. was received by me this evening, by which I learn of the proposed meeting of librarians which convenes tomorrow at the Thousand Islands. You will readily understand that at this late hour I cannot easily arrange to be present there, even were I to presume upon my former connection with this brotherhood for admittance.

One day last week, in unpacking some of my books and papers that have been long stored away, I came upon the original notes of the first Librarians' Convention held thirty-four years ago in New York City. The inception of that gathering was due, if I remember aright, wholly to yourself. I wonder if Friend Guild is not the only one then present who occupies today the same official position he then held. Some few are discharging honorable trusts in other fields, but the great majority have had the inevitable "Finis" inscribed on their completed work.

The Conference was of great interest to those privileged to attend it; and I congratulate you upon being spared and permitted to be in attendance upon this its latest successor.

In the third of a century that has passed since then Bibliography has made great progress, and nowhere greater than in our own country. Here, too, are the finest examples of libraries for the people; with the promise of still more illustrious ones, if that be possible, to come. What nobler foundation can man lay for a monument whereby his memory shall be most gratefully cherished than has been laid by an Astor, a Pratt, a Newberry, a Tilden, and by others less known, but equally true benefactors to the public. And what broad, cultured men will these and our civic and national libraries call for to render such institutions of greatest service to the greatest number. . . .

Yours very sincerely

S. HASTINGS GRANT

Henry Coppée to Charles B. Norton[111]

THE NEPTUNE HOUSE,
OCEAN BEACH, N.J.
Aug. 31, 1887

To General Norton.

MY DEAR GENERAL:

Your kind note and its enclosures came to me in due course. I remember well the meeting of Librarians in New York, in 1853, when I was ex officio the Librarian of West Point.

A generation has passed away and the "day of small things" has also had its sunset. Now our libraries are becoming colossal, and are a power in the land. I wish I could come to the Convention, but I can't. Perhaps it is as well. I belong to that earlier day, and would be more of a curiosity than a help. But I love

books and booklovers and shall look for your proceedings with
great interest.

With sincere regard,

Your friend and servant

H. COPPÉE

As the delegates adjourned and went their way on that
September day in 1853 they doubtless not only expected to
meet again in the near future; they also doubtless believed
that their meeting was destined to have many favorable results on the immediate future of libraries and librarianship.
This editorial in the October number of *Norton's Literary
Gazette*,[112] written a few days after adjournment, probably
by Grant, voiced such hopes:

THE RESULT OF THE LIBRARIANS' CONVENTION

In another portion of our paper we have presented an extended account of the Librarians' Convention, to which in advance we have so often called the attention of our readers. It
will be seen by its perusal that, with very little previous interchange of views upon the subject, and at the mere suggestions
of a dozen Librarians, more than eighty persons interested in
bibliographical and literary matters have assembled from thirteen
different States of the Union. They represent collectively Libraries of more than eight hundred thousand volumes, located
all over our country, from Buffalo to New Orleans, and from
Portland to San Francisco. No one, we think, who attended the
meetings, and no one who reads with care the published proceedings, can doubt that this is the germ of very important results. The acknowledged influence which public Libraries are
to exert upon the people of this country, who are taught in our
extended system of common schools to enjoy and demand the
highest and the freest intellectual advantages; the number of institutions which are already commenced and projected, and the

108

liberal endowments they have occasionally received, alike demand that information should be generally diffused in regard to the best method of forming and maintaining collections of books, both for circulation and reference. This object can only be attained by a comparison of the views and experience of those who are concerned in the management of such institutions. Accordingly, Conventions like that which has just been held are valuable, not merely in proportion to the number of projects which are suggested, nor of the resolutions which are formally adopted, but they must be estimated by the variety, importance, and general applicability of the information which is elicited. Almost every Librarian, however expert, can learn from his neighbors some new ideas; and it is the bounden duty of every new and youthful organization to profit by the history of such societies as are older. It was for this reason that the Convention was originally called, and is hereafter to be held.

The very general nature of the call caused at first some hesitation, in regard to the best manner of organizing the Convention and of conducting its business. It was soon decided, however, that the present meeting should be quite informal in its character, and that, in want of well-matured papers upon various library topics, suggestions and impromptu discussions should be in every way encouraged. The selection of a President of the Convention, and of a Chairman of the Business Committee, who were admirably fitted, by their discrimination and experience, for the duties which were assigned to them, secured method and point to every matter of debate, and greatly facilitated the whole proceedings.

To sum up in a general way the good accomplished by the Convention, we should mention the following more important particulars: Acquaintances have been formed among numerous members of the Librarian's profession, who had never seen or corresponded with one another before; an arrangement has been made for the regular interchange of catalogues and reports; the experience of those who have long had charge of public Libraries has been brought before those who are novices in the work, upon a great variety of topics; the Smithsonian system of cataloguing, which aims at most important changes, has been explained by its originator, and carefully discussed; facts and statistics concerning a large number of widely scattered institutions have been collected and arranged; certain new and ingenious inventions for the preservation and exhibition of illustrated works have been introduced to the public; preliminary steps have been taken for preparing a complete Librarians' Manual; suggestions have been made in regard to the establishment of popular Libraries all over the country; and measures have been taken to form a Librarians' Association, or Bibliographical Society, of a permanent character, the object of which shall be to promote, in every way, the establishment and efficient conduct of collections of books.

Surely a good work has been commenced. It remains for all who are interested in these various particulars, or who desire the highest intellectual advancement of the people at large, to cooperate in the enterprise which is thus begun, and to do what they can, by personal influence and exertion, to secure a large attendance at the next Convention of this kind, in Washington, and to promote the discussion and procure the diffusion of all important facts in relation to Library economy.

The New York *Herald,* on Monday morning, September 19, commented pleasantly and at some length on the Convention, especially encouraging the establishment of more libraries:

When we consider that there are about seven hundred public libraries, exclusive of those connected with schools, in the United States, the necessity of some society for the benefit of librarians, and the still greater extension of libraries, will become obvious. . . . The librarians are confident that with proper and well-directed effort every town and village in the country might be possessed of a library. Several plans having this desirable end in view were suggested, among which we may mention one as particularly deserving of notice. According to this the members are each required to invest a certain amount in money for a library fund, and to contribute an equal number of books. In this way the nucleus of a library might be formed in any village; and by due care and attention, with the aid of its own funds and the fees obtained from its readers we have no doubt that in ninety-nine cases out of a hundred it would be successful. The number of libraries at present established throughout the country might be more than doubled in the course of ten years at the utmost.

After referring to the valuable results hoped for by Jewett's scheme for making catalogs with the use of stereotype plates, which subject was, the article said, next to the establishment of libraries, the most important that claimed consideration, the writer went on to say:

We cannot dismiss this subject without congratulating the members of the Convention on the order, harmony, mutual courtesy, and unanimity, which distinguished their proceedings. It is a rare thing, in this age of woman's rights and temperance conventions, for a body of men to assemble for any specific purpose without being disturbed by angry debates, in which hard names and abuse are freely bestowed by the disputants upon each other. While the same spirit continues to be manifested by the librarians at all their meetings, no apprehensions need be entertained of the success of whatever they may undertake for their own benefit and that of the reading public. We bespeak for them the favor and support of all who wish well to the cause of literature and the diffusion of general information.

The promoters of the Convention secured for it a considerable amount of newspaper publicity. For example, the

New York *Herald* devoted to the proceedings one and a half columns on September 16, two columns on the 17th and one and a half columns on the 19th, in addition to the half column editorial from which we have just quoted. The New York *Tribune* devoted nearly three columns on both the 16th and 17th, and over one column on the 19th. The *Commercial Advertiser,* of New York, gave to the proceedings one and a half columns on the 17th, and the *Post* one column on the same day. The *Times* gave two and a half columns on the 16th and nearly two columns on the 17th. Other New York papers such as the *Journal of Commerce* and the *Morning Courier and Enquirer* gave shorter accounts and comments. The *Providence Journal* of September 20, 21 and 23 contained two and a quarter, one and two-thirds and two-thirds columns respectively in these three issues, all reporting the proceedings, written doubtless by Guild though not signed. Brief announcements or articles of some length appeared in the *Springfield Republican,* the *Baltimore Sun,* the Philadelphia *Public Ledger,* the *Cincinnati Gazette* and doubtless in other papers that have not come to my notice.

All the newspapers were kindly in their attitude toward the Convention and appreciative of the work of libraries and bibliographers. Most of the writers spoke of the unique character of the gathering and of the fact that it was the first convention of librarians ever held.

The notice in the *Tribune* on the opening day of the Convention stressed the professional prominence of those behind the movement. Said the writer, utilizing material printed in *Norton's Literary Gazette,* doubtless furnished to the press by Norton or Grant:

Among the distinguished men who have summoned the Convention are C. C. Jewett, of the Smithsonian Institution, Charles Folsom of the Boston Athenaeum, Samuel F. Haven of the American Antiquarian Society, Barnas Sears of the Massachusetts State Library, E. C. Herrick of Yale College, Joshua Leavitt of the American Geographical and Statistical Society, Edward E. Hale of Worcester, T. W. Harris of Harvard College, and others of high eminence in the department of bibliography. . . . We shall give a full report of the doings of this body, and doubt not that such a unique gathering of literary men will awaken general curiosity and interest.

Most of the newspapers, in one way or another, stated that the general object of the Convention was "to confer upon the means of advancing the prosperity and usefulness of public libraries, and to suggest and discuss topics of interest to book collectors and readers" (The *Tribune,* September 15). Without question more publicity for libraries appeared in the press that week than the subject had ever before received in the history of the world.

Publicity extended as far west as Cincinnati. The *Gazette* of that city, in its issue of Wednesday, September 21, carried a long editorial, probably a direct result of the presence at the Convention of R. H. Stephenson, librarian of the Cincinnati Mercantile Library. The libraries of this country, the editorial began, when compared with the older libraries of Europe, are very imperfect repositories of literature. No collection in America numbers a hundred thousand volumes, and not more than one or two possess half that number. In Europe, every country possessed noble collections of books, varying from one hundred thousand volumes to more than a million. Two things, the writer went on to say, were necessary to the collection of a good library—time and money. In America we had had little of either. For nearly two centuries our few American libraries had grown slowly, from occasional contributions, or from small taxes upon those who enjoyed their use. Generally attached to institutions of learning or appendages to social or beneficiary associations, their object was rather to supply current reading than to make collections valuable to the scholar. The utter inadequacy of these collections for the purpose of historians, political economists or other scholars had repeatedly led to grievous complaints and to the necessity of taking trips to Europe to obtain information which could not be found at home. This discreditable fact had not been without its influence upon benefactors and through their liberality it would perhaps soon cease to be true that no period of American history could be thoroughly investigated in this country. A general spirit of emulation had also been excited, one of the fruits of which had been seen in the proceedings of the Convention last week in New York.

In a country where every State was ambitious to possess a valuable library, where every one of our hundred and fifty colleges must be supplied with its collections of books, and where associations of every kind regard a library as essential to their completeness, there must obviously be many questions to decide, the *Gazette* editorial stated, that could be decided in no other way than by such a body as had just closed its sessions. The Convention had been composed of librarians from all sections of the country, many of them being of widely extended reputation. The resolution to form a permanent association, the writer concluded, was a fortunate one, "as our various public libraries will be stimulated to a healthy competition, and be excited to greater exertions."

This recognition of the utter inadequacy of libraries of this country as they existed in the middle of the nineteenth century is one of the frankest acknowledgments of the situation that had ever appeared in print, and it will not be inappropriate to record this able editorial in the *Cincinnati Gazette* as one of the direct results of the Librarians' Convention.

There were few such *direct* results of this first meeting of librarians. The Convention was, we must admit, just a flash in the pan. But its *indirect* results were many and lasting. Librarians had made contact with each other and formed friendships which proved helpful. Even though they did not meet again in convention for nearly a quarter of a century they corresponded with each other and visited each other's libraries more than they had done previously. They refused to be discouraged by inadequate support or community indifference. They deserve our respect. The delegates to the Librarians' Convention of 1853 were the pioneers of our craft and librarians of later generations should remember them with pride.

Censure, if any, of these men for failing to perform the duty assigned them should be light. They had fallen on trying days for libraries and the gentle art of reading. The clouds of the War between the States were even then gathering on the horizon and they grew steadily in size and blackness until they broke seven and a half years later. Then followed the four terrible years when gatherings were not for the discussion of books or bibliography. After that ten years and more of reconstruction, nearly as barren in literary and educational endeavor and fruitage as those which had gone before. So it was not until twenty-three years after the

Conference of 1853, October 5, 1876, the birthday of the American Library Association, that another meeting of librarians was held.

Appendix

Register of Attendance

The Register is arranged in the order given in *Norton's Literary and Educational Register, for 1854* (p. 50-53), which differs slightly from that given in *Norton's Literary Gazette* (vol. 3, p. 170, Oct. 15, 1853). It is assumed that the *Register* list of delegates is more accurate and complete, since the secretary had more time to check it. In the *Register* list the name of *Ossian Dodge* has been changed to *Robert Dodge,* and the name of J. S. Thayer, of the New York *Evening Post,* has been added. Ossian Euclid Dodge (1820-1876) was at that time editing the *Boston Weekly Museum,* which contains no hint that he attended the Conference; Robert Dodge, however, was living in New York.

Some of the delegates are still so well remembered, at least among librarians, that little more than dates of birth and death and a reference to the *Dictionary of American biography* (hereinafter designated *D.A.B.)* seems to be necessary. Others have been identified in so far as the resources at the editor's disposal have made it possible.

DELEGATES

"The following persons assembled at the rooms of the University of the City of New York, on Thursday, Friday, and Saturday, September 15, 16, and 17, 1853. It will be seen that more than eighty gentlemen were present, the representatives of forty-seven different libraries. These institutions are located in thirteen different states, and contain collectively over six hundred thousand volumes."

Prof. C. C. JEWETT, Librarian of the Smithsonian Institution, *Washington*.

Charles Coffin Jewett, 1816-1868. *(D.A.B.)*

MAINE

JAMES MERRILL, Librarian of the Athenaeum, *Portland*.

James Merrill, 1822-1859, a graduate of Bowdoin College, lawyer and banker.

Prof. ROSWELL D. HITCHCOCK, Bowdoin College, *Brunswick*.

Roswell Dwight Hitchcock, 1817-1887, Congregational clergyman, at that time Professor of Natural and Revealed Religion at Bowdoin College, later Professor of Church History, Union Theological Seminary. *(D.A.B.)*

MASSACHUSETTS

CHARLES FOLSOM, ESQ., Librarian of the Athenaeum, *Boston*.

Charles Folsom, 1794-1872. *(D.A.B.)*

WM. F. POOLE, Librarian of the Mercantile Library Association, *Boston*.

William Frederick Poole, 1821-1894. *(D.A.B.)*

S. F. HAVEN, Librarian of the American Antiquarian Society, *Worcester*.

Samuel Foster Haven, 1806-1881, Librarian of the A.A.S., 1838-1881, historian. (Chas. Deane's *Memoir of Samuel F. Haven, LL.D.* [Cambridge, 1885]; *Memorial of Samuel Foster Haven, LL.D., Librarian of the American Antiquarian Society* [Worcester, 1882].)

Rev. EDW. E. HALE, *Worcester*.

Edward Everett Hale, 1822-1909, clergyman and author. *(D. A.B.)*

RHODE ISLAND

R. A. GUILD, Librarian of Brown University, *Providence*.

Reuben Aldbridge Guild, 1822-1899. *(D.A.B.)*

THOMAS HALE WILLIAMS, Librarian of the Athenaeum, *Providence.*

Thomas Hale Williams, 1814-1901, Librarian of the Providence Athenaeum, 1845-1854; later Librarian of the Minneapolis Athenaeum, which he helped found, for twenty years. *(The [Providence] Athenaeum Bulletin,* vol. 10, no. 2. September 1937.)

ALBERT J. JONES, Director of the Athenaeum, *Providence.*

Albert Jenkins Jones, died in Florence, Italy, in 1887, bequeathing to the Providence Public Library his private library composed largely of Italian and French literature.

CHAS. W. JENCKS, Librarian of the Mechanics' Library, *Providence.*

Charles William Jencks, 1826-1909, head of the Jencks Paper Box Company, Librarian of the Mechanics' Library for the eight years prior to its merging with the Providence Public Library. *(Bulletin of the American Library Association,* vol. 3, p. 132. September 1909.)

CHAS. AKERMAN, Director of the Mechanics' Library, *Providence.*
Charles Akerman, 1812-1879, operated a bindery and manufactured blank books.

S. BALLOU, Carrington Library, *R.I.*

Probably Sullivan Ballou, 1827-1861, a young Providence lawyer, later president of the Park Association there, who lost his life in the Civil War.

CONNECTICUT

Hon. HENRY BARNARD, Superintendent of Common Schools, *Hartford.*

Henry Barnard, 1811-1900, educator. *(D.A.B.)*

HENRY M. BAILEY, Librarian of the Young Men's Institute, *Hartford.*

Henry Mercer Bailey, author of *Thoughts in a Library* (Hartford, 1852) .

DANIEL C. GILMAN, Delegate from the Linonian Library of Yale College, *New Haven.*

Daniel Coit Gilman, 1831-1908. *(D.A.B.)*

Rev. JAS. T. DICKINSON, *Durham.*

James Taylor Dickinson, 1806-1884, a Congregational minister.

NEW YORK CITY AND STATE

PHILIP J. FORBES, ESQ., Librarian of the New York Society Library, *New York.*

Philip Jones Forbes, 1807-1877, Librarian from 1828 to 1855, and later in the book business.

GEO. H. MOORE, Librarian of the New York Historical Society, *New York.*

George Henry Moore, 1823-1892. *(D.A.B.)*

Prof. HENRY B. SMITH, D.D., Librarian of the Union Theological Seminary, *New York.*

Henry Boynton Smith, 1815-1877, Professor of Church History and Theology, Librarian, Union Theological Seminary, 1850-1874. *(D.A.B.)*

J. L. LYONS, Assistant Librarian of the Union Theological Seminary, *New York.*

Jerre Lorenzo Lyons, 1824-1888, then a student at Union Theological Seminary.

WM. CURTIS NOYES, ESQ., Librarian of the New York Law Institute, *New York.*

William Curtis Noyes, 1805-1864, distinguished lawyer who left his fine library to Hamilton College. *(D.A.B.)*

WM. A. JONES, Librarian of Columbia College, *New York.*

William Alfred Jones, 1817-1900, Librarian of Columbia from 1851 to 1865, author and essayist. *(D.A.B.)*

JOHN L. VANDERVOORT, M.D., Librarian of the New York Hospital, *New York.*

John Ledyard Vandervoort, 1809-1891, Librarian from 1837 until his death. *(Medical Record, vol. 40, p. 104. July, 1891.)*

Prof. HOWARD CROSBY, Librarian of the University of the City of New York.

Howard Crosby, 1826-1891, Presbyterian clergyman, Professor of Greek, 1851-1859, author. *(D.A.B.)*

JAMES HENRY, JR., Actuary of the Mechanics' Institute, *New York.*

WM. OLAND BOURNE, Assistant Librarian of the Free Academy, *New York.*

Author of several volumes of poetry, and *History of the Public School Society of the City of New York* (1870).

E. A. HARRIS, Librarian of the American Institute, *New York.*

Ezekiel A. Harris, 1831-1924?, survived all other members of the Conference.

S. HASTINGS GRANT, Librarian of the Mercantile Library, *New York.*

Seth Hastings Grant, 1828-1910. *(New York Genealogical and Biographical Record,* vol. 42, p. 1-6. January, 1911.)

WM. VAN NORDEN, Representative of the Apprentices' Library, *New York.*

William Van Norden died in 1871 after several years of service.

HENRY GITTERMAN, Assistant Librarian of the Hebrew Young Men's Literary Association, *New York.*

J. DISTURNELL, Member of the American Geographical and Statistical Society, *New York.*

John Disturnell, 1801-1877, author and compiler of guide books, Librarian of the Cooper Union, 1865-1870. *(D.A.B.)*

Rev. ISAAC FERRIS, D.D., Chancellor of the University of the City of New York.

Isaac Ferris, 1798-1873. *(D.A.B.)*

Rev. THOMAS DEWITT, D.D., Vice President of the New York Historical Society, *New York.*

Thomas DeWitt, 1791-1874, Dutch Reformed clergyman, for nearly fifty years pastor of the Collegiate Church and public figure in New York. *(National Cyclopedia of American Biography,* vol. 2, p. 434.)

DANIEL W. FISKE, Assistant Librarian of the Astor Library, *New York*.

Daniel Willard Fiske, 1831-1904, Librarian of Cornell University, 1868-1883, book collector and scholar, bequeathed his collections of Dante, Petrarch and Icelandic literature to Cornell, together with a large endowment. *(D.A.B.)*

MAUNSELL B. FIELD, ESQ., Recording Secretary of the New York Historical Society, *New York*.

Maunsell Bradhurst Field, 1822-1875, lawyer, author and civil servant. *(D.A.B.)*

EDWIN WILLIAMS, of the Library Committee of the American Institute, *New York*.

Edwin Williams, 1797-1854, author of many historical books and manuals, journalist. *(D.A.B.)*

Rev. GORHAM D. ABBOTT, Principal of the Spingler Institute, *New York*.

Gorham Dummer Abbott, 1807-1874, clergyman chiefly interested in the education of girls, founder of the Spingler Institute, which, under his leadership, became very well known. *(D.A.B.)*

Prof. BENJ. N. MARTIN, University of the City of New York.

Benjamin Nicholas Martin, 1816-1883, Professor of Intellectual Philosophy, History and Belles Lettres, University of the City of New York, 1853-1883. *(Cyclopedia of American Biographies.)*

Prof. JOHN TORREY, of the College of Physicians and Surgeons, *New York*.

John Torrey, 1796-1873, botanist and chemist, preceptor of Asa Gray. *(D.A.B.)*

Rev. SAMUEL OSGOOD, Delegate from the Providence Athenaeum.

Samuel Osgood, 1812-1880, was listed in the *Gazette* as from Providence, where he had held a pastorate. Actually he had been living in New York since 1849, when he became pastor of the Church of the Messiah. Popular preacher and author. *(National Cyclopedia of American Biography, vol. 9, p. 236.)*

Wm. C. Gilman, Esq., *New York.*

William Charles Gilman, 1795-1863, father of Daniel Coit Gilman, business man of many interests, charitable and religious. (Arthur Gilman's *The Gilman Family* [1869], p. 133-144.)

Prof. George W. Greene, *New York.*

George Washington Greene, 1811-1883, historian, lecturer, biographer and friend of Longfellow. *(D.A.B.)*

Rev. E. H. Chapin, *New York.*

Edwin Hubbell Chapin, 1814-1880, Universalist clergyman, noted for his eloquence, love of humanity, and many books. *(D.A.B.)*

John Banvard, *New York.*

John Banvard, 1815-1891, painter and traveler. *(D.A.B.)*

Charles B. Norton, Literary Gazette, *New York.*

Charles Benjamin Norton, 1825-1891, promoter of the Conference. *(Cyclopedia of American Biographies.)*

Aug. Maverick, New York Times.

Augustus Maverick, reporter and author of *Henry J. Raymond and the New York Times* (1870).

J. W. Kennady, New York Express.

J. S. Thayer, Evening Post, *New York.*

John J. Schroeder, *New York.*

Edwin H. Grant, M.D., *New York.*

Edwin Hodges Grant, 1831-   , brother of S. Hastings Grant.

S. S. Purple, M.D., *New York.*

Samuel Smith Purple, 1822-1900, physician, genealogist and book collector. *(D.A.B.)*

Mr. Perry, of the Astor Library, *New York.*

Probably one of the two Assistant Librarians, referred to in the Annual Report.

Robert Dodge, *New York.*

Robert Dodge, 1820-1899, lawyer and author. *(Cyclopedia of American Biographies.)*

Aug. K. Gardner, M.D., *New York.*

Augustus Kinsley Gardner, 1821-1876, member of the N. Y. Academy of Medicine and author of several books.

Thomas J. Sawyer, *New York.*

Thomas Jefferson Sawyer, 1804-1899, Universalist clergyman. *(D.A.B.)*

Joseph F. Noyes, Librarian of the Athenaeum, *Brooklyn.*

Joseph F. Noyes was the first librarian of the Brooklyn Athenaeum, which had been established just the year before the Conference.

George H. Stebbins, Principal of Public Schools, *Brooklyn.*

George H. Stebbins, 1819-   , for several years principal of schools in Brooklyn. (R. S. Greenslee's *The Stebbins Genealogy* [1904], vol. 2, p. 1155.)

Harold Hinde, *Brooklyn.*

Capt. Henry Coppée, Librarian of the U. S. Military, *West Point.*

Henry Coppée, 1821-1895, Assistant Professor of Geography, History and Ethics, as well as Librarian; later President of Lehigh University, author of several textbooks, histories and biographies. *(D.A.B.)*

Prof. A. J. Upson, Librarian of Hamilton College, *Clinton.*

Anson Judd Upson, 1823-1902, Professor of Rhetoric and Moral Philosophy, Hamilton College, 1849-1870, later Chancellor of the University of the State of New York. *(National Cyclopedia of American Biography,* vol. 4, p. 489.)

H. P. Filer, Librarian of the Young Men's Association, *Troy.*

Henry P. Filer, Librarian, 1846-1864, son of Zephaniah Filer, the first librarian of the old "Troy Library."

W. T. Willard, Librarian of the Lyceum of Natural History, *Troy.*

William Tell Willard, 1796-

Elias S. Hawley, Representative of the Young Men's Association, *Buffalo.*

Elias Sill Hawley, 1812-1899, lawyer, formerly Superintendent of Public Schools, genealogist and compiler of *The Hawley Record*

(1890). *(New England Historical and Genealogical Register,* vol. 54, p. cxxix-cxxx.)

C. H. RAYMOND, *Buffalo.*

Prof. G. M. GIGER, Librarian of the College of New Jersey, *Princeton.*

George Musgrave Giger, 1822-1865.

Prof. W. HENRY GREEN, Librarian of the Theological Seminary, *Princeton.*

William Henry Green, 1825-1900, Professor of Biblical and Oriental Literature, author of several scholarly books. *(D.A.B.)*

F. W. RICORD, Librarian of the New Library Association, *Newark.*

Frederick William Ricord, 1819-1897, Librarian from 1849 to 1869, public official, and Librarian of the New Jersey Historical Society, 1881-1897. *(D.A.B.)*

Rev. C. R. V. ROMONDT, Librarian of Rutgers College, *New Brunswick.*

Charles R. Von Romondt, a Dutch Reformed minister ordained in 1844.

S. G. DEETH, *New Brunswick,* and *Washington, D. C.*

Sylvanus G. Deeth, a bookseller, and court reporter, whose library was sold at auction in 1860.

WM. COOPER, *Hoboken.*

William Cooper, 1798?-1864, later Vice President of the Lyceum of Natural History (now New York Academy of Sciences) and on its publication committee, paleontologist.

PENNSYLVANIA

LLOYD P. SMITH, Librarian of the Library Company, *Philadelphia.*

Lloyd Pearsall Smith, 1822-1886, one of the charter members of the American Library Association. *(D.A.B.)*

JOHN WM. WALLACE, Librarian of the Law Association, *Philadelphia*.

John William Wallace, 1815-1884, legal scholar and historian, named librarian of the Law Association in 1841. *(D.A.B.)*

MARYLAND

JAMES GREEN, Librarian of the Mercantile Library Association, *Baltimore*.

A. C. RHODES, Vice President of the Mercantile Library Association, *Baltimore*.

OHIO

ELIJAH HAYWARD, Librarian of the State Library, *Columbus*.

Elijah Hayward, 1786-1864, State Librarian of Ohio 1852-1855, lawyer, judge and historian. (New England Historic Genealogical Society. *Memorial Biographies*, vol. 6, p. 41-47.)

R. H. STEPHENSON, Librarian of the Mercantile Library Association, *Cincinnati*.

Reuben Henry Stephenson, 1822-1881, Librarian, 1852-1860.

MISSOURI

W. P. CURTIS, Librarian of the Mercantile Library Association, *St. Louis*.

FREDERIC VINTON, *St. Louis*.

Frederic Vinton, 1817-1900, was then cataloging his brother Alfred's private library, in 1856 he became assistant librarian in the Boston Public Library, in 1865 first assistant librarian of the Library of Congress, and in 1873 Librarian of Princeton University; one of the charter members of the American Library Association. *(D.A.B.)*

LOUISIANA

JOHN L. SHEAFE, Librarian of the State Library of Louisiana, *New Orleans*.

B. F. FRENCH, Representative of the Fisk Free Library, *New Orleans*.

Benjamin Franklin French, 1799-1877, one of the founders of the Fisk Free Library, then, however, a resident in New York City. *(National Cyclopedia of American Biography*, vol. 3, p. 522.)

CALIFORNIA

EDWARD E. DUNBAR, Delegate from the Mercantile Library Association, *San Francisco*.

Edward Ely Dunbar, 1818-1871, one of the directors of the Mercantile Library which had been opened March 1st. (Moses S. Beach's *The Ely Ancestry* [1902], p. 383-384.)

Proceedings of the Librarians' Convention
Held in New York City, September 15, 16, and 17, 1853

(Reprinted by photo-offset from
Norton's Literary and Educational
Register, for 1854)

PROCEEDINGS

OF THE

LIBRARIANS' CONVENTION,

HELD IN NEW YORK CITY, SEPT. 15, 16, AND 17, 1853.

CALL.

THE undersigned, believing that the knowledge of Books, and the foundation and management of collections of them for public use, may be promoted by consultation and concert among librarians and others interested in bibliography, respectfully invite such persons to meet IN CONVENTION AT NEW YORK, ON THURSDAY, THE FIFTEENTH DAY OF SEPTEMBER, for the purpose of conferring together upon the means of advancing the prosperity and usefulness of public libraries, and for the suggestion and discussion of topics of importance to book collectors and readers.
MAY, 1853.

CHAS. FOLSOM, *Boston Athenæum.*
C. C. JEWETT, *Smithsonian Institution.*
T. W. HARRIS, *Harvard College.*
PHILIP J. FORBES, *Society Library, N. Y.*
SAMUEL F. HAVEN, *American Antiquarian Society.*
BARNAS SEARS, *Massachusetts State Library.*
E. C. HERRICK, *Yale College.*
JOSHUA LEAVITT, *American Geographical and Statistical Society.*
EDWARD E. HALE, *Worcester, Mass.*
HENRY BARNARD, *Hartford, Ct.*

J. W. CHAMBERS, *American Institute.*
WM. E. JILLSON, *Providence, R. I.*
A. J. UPSON, *Hamilton College.*
JAMES GREEN, *Baltimore Mercantile Library.*
W. A. JONES, *Columbia College.*
R. A. GUILD, *Brown University.*
G. H. MOORE, *New York Historical Society.*
W. F. POOLE, *Boston Mercantile Library.*
N. B. SHURTLEFF, *American Academy of Arts and Sciences.*
S. HASTINGS GRANT, *New York Mercantile Library.*
L. M. BOLTWOOD, *Amherst College.*
WM. P. CURTIS, *St. Louis Mercantile Library.*
R. H. STEPHENSON, *Cincinnati Mercantile Library.*
H. M. BAILEY, *Hartford Young Men's Institute.*
GEO. E. DAY, *Lane Seminary.*
LLOYD P. SMITH, *Philadelphia Library Company.*

DELEGATES.

In accordance with the foregoing call, the following persons assembled at the rooms of the University of the City of New York, on Thursday, Friday, and Saturday, Sept. 15, 16, and 17, 1853. It will be seen that more than eighty gentlemen were present, the representatives of forty-seven different libraries. These institutions are located in thirteen different States, and contain collectively over six hundred thousand volumes.

DISTRICT OF COLUMBIA.

Prof. C. C. JEWETT, Librarian of the Smithsonian Institution, *Washington.*

MAINE.

JAMES MERRILL, Librarian of the Athenæum, *Portland.*
Prof. ROSWELL D. HITCHCOCK, Bowdoin College, *Brunswick.*

MASSACHUSETTS.

CHARLES FOLSOM, Esq., Librarian of the Athenæum, *Boston.*
WM. F. POOLE, Librarian of the Mercantile Library Association, *Boston.*
S. F. HAVEN, Librarian of the American Antiquarian Society, *Worcester.*
Rev. EDW. E. HALE, *Worcester.*

R. A. GUILD, Librarian of Brown University, *Providence.*
THOMAS HALE WILLIAMS, Librarian of the Athenæum, *Providence.*
ALBERT J. JONES, Director of the Athenæum, *Providence.*
CHAS. W. JENCKS, Librarian of the Mechanics' Library, *Providence.*
CHAS. AKERMAN, Director of the Mechanics' Library, *Providence.*
S. BALLOU, Carrington Library, *R. I.*

CONNECTICUT.

Hon. HENRY BARNARD, Superintendent of Common Schools, *Hartford.*
HENRY M. BAILEY, Librarian of the Young Men's Institute, *Hartford.*
DANIEL C. GILMAN, Delegate from the Linonian Library of Yale College, *New Haven.*
Rev. JAS. T. DICKINSON, *Durham.*

NEW YORK CITY AND STATE.

PHILIP J. FORBES, Esq., Librarian of the New York Society Library, *New York.*
GEO. H. MOORE, Librarian of the New York Historical Society, *New York.*
Prof. HENRY B. SMITH, D. D., Librarian of the Union Theological Seminary, *New York.*
J. L. LYONS, Assistant Librarian of the Union Theological Seminary, *New York.*
WM. CURTIS NOYES, Esq., Librarian of the New York Law Institute, *New York.*
WM. A. JONES, Librarian of Columbia College, *New York.*
JOHN L. VANDERVOORT, M. D., Librarian of the New York Hospital, *New York.*
Prof. HOWARD CROSBY, Librarian of the University of the City of New York.
JAMES HENRY, Jr., Actuary of the Mechanics' Institute, *New York.*
WM. OLAND BOURNE, Assistant Librarian of the Free Academy, *New York.*
E. A. HARRIS, Librarian of the American Institute, *New York.*
S. HASTINGS GRANT, Librarian of the Mercantile Library, *New York.*
WM. VAN NORDEN, Representative of the Apprentices' Library, *New York.*
HENRY GITTERMAN, Assistant Librarian of the Hebrew Young Men's Literary Association, *New York.*

J. Disturnell, Member of the American Geographical and Statistical Society, *New York.*

Rev. Isaac Ferris, D. D., Chancellor of the University of the City of New York.

Rev. Thomas De Witt, D. D., Vice President of the New York Historical Society, *New York.*

Daniel W. Fiske, Assistant Librarian of the Astor Library, *New York.*

Maunsell B. Field, Esq., Recording Secretary of the New York Historical Society, *New York.*

Edwin Williams, of the Library Committee of the American Institute, *New York.*

Rev. Gorham D. Abbott, Principal of the Spingler Institute, *New York.*

Prof. Benj. N. Martin, University of the City of New York.

Prof. John Torrey, of the College of Physicians and Surgeons, *New York.*

Rev. Samuel Osgood, Delegate from the Providence Athenæum.

Wm. C. Gilman, Esq., *New York.*

Prof. George W. Greene, *New York.*

Rev. E. H. Chapin, *New York.*

John Banvard, *New York.*

Charles B. Norton, Literary Gazette, *New York.*

Aug. Maverick, New York Times.

J. W. Kennady, New York Express.

J. S. Thayer, Evening Post, *New York.*

John J. Schroeder, *New York.*

Edwin H. Grant, M. D., *New York.*

S. S. Purple, M. D., *New York.*

Mr. Perry, of the Astor Library, *New York.*

Robert Dodge, *New York.*

Aug. K. Gardner, M. D., *New York.*

Thomas J. Sawyer, *New York.*

Joseph F. Noyes, Librarian of the Athenæum, *Brooklyn.*

Geo. H. Stebbins, Principal of Public Schools, *Brooklyn.*

Harold Hinde, *Brooklyn.*

Capt. Henry Coppée, Librarian of the U. S. Military Academy, *West Point.*

Prof. A. J. Upson, Librarian of Hamilton College, *Clinton.*

H. P. Filer, Librarian of the Young Men's Association, *Troy.*

W. T. Willard, Librarian of the Lyceum of Natural History, *Troy.*

134

ELIAS S. HAWLEY, Representative of the Young Men's Association, *Buffalo.*
C. H. RAYMOND, *Buffalo.*

Prof. G. M. GIGER, Librarian of the College of New Jersey, *Princeton.*
Prof. W. HENRY GREEN, Librarian of the Theological Seminary, *Princeton.*
F. W. RICORD, Librarian of the Newark Library Association, *Newark.*
Rev. C. R. V. ROMONDT, Librarian of Rutgers College, *New Brunswick.*
S. G. DEETH, *New Brunswick,* and *Washington, D. C.*
WM. COOPER, *Hoboken.*

PENNSYLVANIA.

LLOYD P. SMITH, Librarian of the Library Company, *Philadelphia.*
JOHM WM. WALLACE, Librarian of the Law Association, *Philadelphia.*

MARYLAND.

JAMES GREEN, Librarian of the Mercantile Library Association, *Baltimore.*
A. C. RHODES, Vice President of the Mercantile Library Association, *Baltimore.*

OHIO.

ELIJAH HAYWARD, Librarian of the State Library, *Columbus.*
R. H. STEPHENSON, Librarian of the Mercantile Library Association, *Cincinnati.*

MISSOURI.

W. P. CURTIS, Librarian of the Mercantile Library Association, *St. Louis.*
FREDERICK VINTON, *St. Louis.*

LOUISIANA.

JOHN L. SHEAFE, Librarian of the State Library of Louisiana, *New Orleans.*
B. F. FRENCH, Representative of the Fisk Free Library, *New Orleans.*

CALIFORNIA.

EDWARD E. DUNBAR, Delegate from the Mercantile Library Association, *San Francisco.*

Apologies were also presented from the following gentlemen, unable to be present:—

Dr. Cogswell, of the Astor Library; Prof. Beck, of the N. Y. State Library; Dr. Harris, of Harvard College Library; E. C. Herrick, Esq., of Yale College Library; Dr. Sears, of the Massachusetts State Library; George Livermore, Esq., of Boston; Prof. Johnson, of the N. Y. State Agricultural Society; Rev. Adolph Frost, of the Burlington (N. J.) College Library, and Wm. MacDermott, of Norristown Library, Pa.

OFFICERS.

The Convention was called to order by Charles Folsom, Esq., of the Boston Athenæum, and, upon motion, the following persons were chosen officers :

President :

Prof. CHAS. C. JEWETT, Smithsonian Institution, Washington, D. C.

Secretary :

S. HASTINGS GRANT, Mercantile Library Association, New York City.

Business Committee:

CHARLES FOLSOM, Athenæum, Boston,
PHILIP J. FORBES, Society Library, New York,
J. W. WALLACE, Law Association, Philadelphia,
R. A. GUILD, Brown University, Providence,
R. H. STEPHENSON, Mercantile Library Association, Cincinnati,
With the President and Secretary of the Convention.

OPENING ADDRESS OF THE PRESIDENT.

Prof. JEWETT, upon taking the chair, acknowledged the honor conferred upon him, and proceeded to remark as follows :

It must be highly gratifying to those who signed the call for this Convention, to notice the response which it, this morning, receives. To every one who knows the nature of a librarian's duties,—the details which consume his days, and render absence from his post impossible, except at the cost of severe labor on his return,—it must be manifest that we have met at considerable personal sacrifice. We obey some strong and wide-felt impulse in incurring the expense and the trouble of this gathering.

The call for this Convention was not the result of a correspondence among librarians, nor was it the subject of long and careful consideration. It was, rather, a spontaneous movement. It was first, I think, suggested a year ago, or more, in the Literary Gazette. Librarians spoke to each other on the matter, when they happened to meet. Every one was pleased with the idea. At length a formal call was written, and signed by a few who happened to meet the gentlemen having charge of the paper.

In compliance with such an invitation, we have assembed this morning. It is not, so far as I know, proposed to accomplish any end by this Convention, beyond the general one expressed in the call, of "conferring together upon the means of advancing the prosperity and usefulness of public libraries," and of seeking mutual instruction and encouragement in the discharge of the quiet and unostentatious labors of our vocation, for which each, at his separate post, finds perhaps but little sympathy— for which each, when at home, must derive enthusiasm only from within himself, and from the silent masters of his daily communion.

We have no peculiar views to present, no particular set of measures to propose. We meet without preparation. No order of business has been arranged. Our proceedings must be spontaneous as our meeting. It is not important that they be systematic and formal. We come to receive and to act upon suggestions. We are not here for stately debate, for conspicuous action, much less for an exhibition of ourselves. These things are foreign from our vocation, and not congenial with our tastes. We meet for familiar, informal, conversational conference, where each may take his part, and no one be prevented from contributing his share to the profits of the enterprise, by his inexperience in public speaking, or his inability to make elaborate preparation. Those gentlemen connected with the public press who honor us with their presence, must have been attracted hither by a scholarlike sympathy with our quiet pursuits, which will lead them to appreciate our feelings in this respect, in the reports which they may give.

It is indeed to be hoped that our meeting will have its influence upon the public mind. If our discussions are natural and unrestrained, suggested and shaped by right views of the position which we hold, or ought to hold, in general society and in the republic of letters; if they present to ourselves and to others the difficulties with which we have to contend; if they elicit thought and information upon the collecting of books for private culture, for public enlightenment, and for learned investigations, and upon the best means of promoting the increase and efficiency of such collections;—if we manifest here, while we talk of books as material objects, and of books in their internal significance, that respectful, dignified, and noiseless spirit inspired by the associations in the midst of

which we live, the public will certainly feel and acknowledge the beneficial influence of our meeting, and will desire an official report of the
progress and results of our deliberations.

The occasion is one of peculiar interest. This is the first convention
of the kind, not only in this country, but, so far as I know, in the world.

There have, indeed, been bibliographical associations, but they have
been, for the most part, composed of *dilettante*, and not of practical
librarians and lovers of books. The gratification of a passion for rare
and curious books has generally been their object. Books were too
often valuable to them, only as they were worthless to the rest of the
world. Each member glorying in the possession of a unique copy of
some old work, was required to reprint it, with only copies enough to give
one to each member. One society has played the part of *bibliotaph*, by
requiring, that if a member dies, and his copy of one of these reprints is
to be sold by auction, it shall be bought by the Society at any price it
may be necessary to pay.

These associations have had their origin in a different state of society
from ours. We can at present have but little sympathy with their principal design. We have none whatever with their selfishness.

We would not be supposed to chide the passion for book rarities, where
it exhibits itself simply in collecting and preserving what is curious and
costly, and not in its destruction or concealment. Why should not a
rich man spend his money in this way, as well as in a thousand others
which are harmless? We may go further, and assert that a collection
of rare books can scarcely be formed, without subserving the interests
of learning, whether made with such a design or not. The public are
not unfrequently surprised by results anticipated only by the collector.

I may allude, in this connection, to a distinguished gentleman in our
own country, who made, at great expense, a collection of early-printed
books, without any regard to the subjects of which they treated, the
languages in which they were written, or their worth as literary productions. By those who did not know his purpose, he was called a *bibliomaniac*. He had, however, a definite object in view, which was, to
investigate the early history of typography by its monuments. Books
which he never cared to read, were full of instruction to him. He deduced from the close examination of them, many facts new to the bibliographical world, and showed the unsoundness of many generally received
theories. For example, he satisfied himself that books, in the early days
of typography, were never printed from block letters, that is, from sepa-

rate types of wood, or of wood faced with metal. He proved, too, that many of these books were printed one page at a time. It had been supposed that the early printers must have had immense fonts of type. In many folios the sheets are quired, and it was very naturally supposed that the type of every page of the quire must have been set up before any was printed off. But he traced a broken letter from page to page, and he found such irregularities of register as could not have occurred, had the two pages of the same form been printed at the same time; and he thus demonstrated that these books were printed page by page, and that consequently only a very small font of type was necessary.

Now, these are new, interesting, and valuable results; and they are only specimens which occur to me at the moment, of deductions from the examination of books, which an ordinary observer would say it was infatuation to collect.

But our object, at present, is of a more manifestly and eminently practical and utilitarian character. We meet to provide for the diffusion of a knowledge of good books, and for enlarging the means of public access to them. Our wishes are for the public, not for ourselves.

In our assembling to-day we obey the impulses of our peculiar civilization. We are preëminently a reading people. In Prussia the whole population are taught to read; but a distinguished citizen of that country, who had traveled in the United States, once expressed to me the difference between his own countrymen and the Americans, by saying: "Our people *can* read, your people *do* read." The generally diffused love of reading, for the sake of gaining information, has led to the establishment of a large number of libraries, so that, in the number and general diffusion of small collections of books, we are richer already than any other country in the world. Reading creates the desire to read more, and select reading increases the desire to read profitably. Hence, in every village the questions are asked: "How shall we get good books? How shall we keep them? How shall we use them?" To consult on the best replies to questions like these, is one of the objects of our assembling to-day.

Another demand of our peculiar civilization is, for the means of thorough and independent investigation. We wish to own no men as masters. We intend to re-examine all history from our own American stand point, and we must rewrite it, where we find its facts have been tortured to teach the doctrines of injustice and oppression. The mental activity of this country is surveying every field of research, literary,

8*

scientific, æsthetic, industrial, and philanthropic. It requires to know what others have done and thought, that it may itself press farther outward. This country, therefore, demands the means of the amplest research, and this demand must and will be met.

These views have impressed themselves deeply upon our minds, as we are the appointed custodians of the literary treasures of the country, and have led us to desire mutual assistance and concentration of efforts in providing for these intellectual necessities of our American life. For our present meeting it has been proposed to adopt the simplest form of organization; to appoint, besides a president and a secretary, a business committee to receive suggestions and propositions, and arrange the order of proceedings for each day's session. I unite most cordially in the hope which I have heard expressed this morning, that this Convention may be the precursor of a permanent and highly useful association.

COURTESIES.

Invitations were received and accepted to visit the following libraries: Astor, Society, Historical, Union, Theological, Columbia College, Mercantile, American Institute, Mechanics' Institute, and Free Academy; also from the Directors of the Crystal Palace, through T. Sedgwick, Esq., to visit the Exhibition of Industry; from Mr. Bryan, to the Gallery of Christian Art; from Dr. Abbott, to the Museum of Egyptian Antiquities; and from Mr. Banvard, to his Panorama of the Holy Land.

An invitation to a social gathering at the Kemble House was also presented by members of the Convention from the city of New York.

REPORTS FROM LIBRARIES.

Early in the Convention, reports were presented by the different librarians present, in regard to the condition of the institutions in their charge. These returns have been incorporated, in an afterpart of this Register, with recent information received from other libraries.

Among other remarks, the following were made by Capt. Coppée, in regard to the Library of the United States Military Academy, at West Point.

MR. PRESIDENT AND GENTLEMEN OF THE CONVENTION:

The Institution which I have the honor to represent is certainly peculiar and unique—both *sui juris* and *sui generis*—in that it is under the control of the general government, and that its special character is military and scientific.

You have read the "*Médecin malgré lui ;*" I may truly say that when I was appointed Librarian of the Military Academy, I was a librarian in spite of myself. The little service I had seen, and the partial fondness for certain kinds of reading, had given me no knowledge of the great progressive science of bibliography, a science nobler in its results than simple authorship, in that it classifies and makes available at one intelligent glance, masses of matter, rich specimens of mental ore, which otherwise would lie hidden and useless to the world.

What, however, was received with reluctance, has been retained with pleasure, and pursued with such ardor as the pressure of other duties would permit.

The library of the Military Academy is sustained and increased by an appropriation of $1,000 a year, which, I regret to be obliged to say, is found insufficient to keep pace with the valuable publications in our special branches. Some years, owing to a spirit of retrenchment in Congress, this inadequate sum has been intermitted, and then, in military phrase, we "mark time" for a year, which is, in effect, retrograding to an alarming degree. "Not to advance," says a good maxim, "is to fall back :" the individual student and the public library alike verify its truth.

When the appointment of Librarian was conferred upon me, I found that, with a rigor at once ill-judged and ill-productive, almost all light literature,—poetry, fiction and some of those charming modern works, which, verily, can only be characterized as lying between the two,—a delectable land of the heart and the imagination,—had been interdicted. Since that time, careful additions of standard works of these classes have been made : we ventured, sir, upon a set of the Waverley Novels, and introduced the Corps of Cadets to the Great Magician—need I add, with perfect satisfaction to all concerned.

I have one word to add in favor of a popular direction to our proceedings. It is in accordance with the pervading spirit of our government. The people, sir, are the rule ; everything else, the exception.

Let our deliberations, then, not lose sight of this fact. Rare books cost great prices, and are read afterwards by few,—the scholars, the great book-makers for future generations—and these should not be neglected; but, first remember, that good current learning and knowledge, facts and practical science for the million are within the reach of small sums, the assessment of which will scarcely be felt by the poorest, and the aggregate of which will astonish the people by its greatness, and enlighten the world by its influence.

THE SMITHSONIAN INSTITUTION, AND ITS PLAN OF CATALOGUING.

Mr. Haven, of Worcester, having been called to the Chair, an exposition was made in regard to the Smithsonian Institution at Washington, by Prof. Charles C. Jewett.

He first presented the following table, which exhibits the number of books and other articles added to the library of the Smithsonian Institution during the year 1852, with the sources from which they were received:—

	Books.	Pamph.	Parts.	Eng'gs.	Maps.	Music.	Drawings.	Other Articles.	Totals.
By Purchase, . .	641	918	1568	—	—	—	—	—	3127
By Donations, .	1481	1935	171	10	1698	—	—	41	5336
By Copyright, .	476	96	26	15	10	692	9	19	1343
Totals,	2598	2949	1765	25	1708	692	9	60	9806

The extent of the various collections in the library, at the end of 1852, is shown by the following table:—

	Books.	Pamph.	Parts.	Eng'gs.	Maps.	Musc.	Drawings.	Other Articles.	Totals.
By Purchase, . .	3873	957	1568	1335	2	—	—	—	7735
By Donations, .	2657	3872	171	58	1725	—	30	41	8554
By Copyright, .	2304	213	26	24	51	1826	9	86	4539
By Deposit, . .	873	—	—	—	—	—	—	—	873
Totals,	9707	5042	1765	1417	1778	1826	39	127	21701

In answer to various inquiries, Prof. Jewett also stated in this connection, that the average number of books annually received under the copyright law was about 450. He presumed that this was not more than one-third of all the books copyrighted in the country. The laws regulating the deposit were defective. One copy is required to be deposited with the District Clerk and by him to be transmitted to the Department of State at Washington; one copy is also required to be deposited in the Library of Congress, and one in the Library of the Smithsonian Institution. A larger number of these books is probably received at the Smithsonian Institution than in either of the other libraries. The deposit in the State Department is regarded as burdensome, and the President, in a recent message, recommended that the copyright business be transferred from the Department. There ought to be somewhere a complete collection of these books, as there is of models of machines in the Patent Office. The protection of authors and publishers requires that certified copies of their publications should be preserved. The public have also a great interest in providing that one copy of everything issued from the press should be preserved for future reference. It was hoped that some modifications of the present laws might be made, which would secure both these ends and at the same time diminish the present requirements from publishers. No provision was made by law for transmitting these books to the places of deposit. Consequently many of those deposited with the District Clerks never reach the State Department. Some of those sent to the Smithsonian Institution, cost twenty times what they are worth, being sent, by mail, sealed, by publishers who suppose that the Institution possesses the franking privilege.

Prof. JEWETT then proceeded as follows:—

It is well known to you, Mr. Chairman, and to other gentlemen present, that previous to the passage of the act of Congress establishing the Smithsonian Institution, various propositions were from time to time made to Congress, for the appropriation of the fund bequeathed to the United States by James Smithson, "to found at Washington an establishment for the increase and diffusion of knowledge among men." One project was to establish an astronomical observatory, another to form an agricultural school, another to found a National University, another to place the money under the charge of the National Institute, &c., &c. No one of the many plans suggested met the approval of Congress, until Mr. Choate proposed, and in one of his most brilliant and effective speeches advocated, the establishment of a great central library of reference and research. His bill met with general approval and passed the Senate, but was lost among other unfinished business in the lower House. At the next session of Congress, a select committee was appointed by the House of Representatives, upon the administration of the Smithsonian trust. The members of this committee were divided in opinion. They finally reported a bill, in which the Library was a subordinate but still an important feature. When this bill came up for discussion, Mr. Choate's plan was vigorously attacked by one of the leading members of the committee; but it found powerful advocates. Mr. Marsh defended the library in a speech of great learning, ability and eloquence. So strongly did the House approve of Mr. Marsh's views, that when he introduced a series of amendments, designed, as he expressly stated, "to direct the appropriation entirely to the purpose of a library," everything which he proposed was adopted. Congress refused to limit the annual appropriation for the Library to 10,000, or even to 20,000 dollars. By fixing the maximum of the annual appropriation at $25,000, a sum nearly equal to the whole income of the fund, Congress unequivocally indicated its intentions, had they not been made sufficiently clear by other votes.

The principal management of the Institution was intrusted to a Board of Regents, composed of three Senators, three Representatives, six citizens of the States, appointed by joint resolution, and three members ex-officio, namely, the Vice President of the United States, the Chief Justice of the Supreme Court, and the Mayor of the City of Washington. It was soon found that there were two prominent parties in the Board—not hostile parties, for there is nothing hostile in such matters, but parties of different views in reference to the objects to be pursued by the Institution. One party was in favor of adhering to the library plan, stamped as it was with the approval of Congress; the other was in favor of expending the income in publications and scientific researches. After considerable discussion, it was agreed to divide the income of the Institution permanently between the two great departments : that of collections in literature, science and art, and that of publications and scientific researches.

This plan was followed for a time, but at present a large proportion of the fund is appropriated to other purposes than those of the Library. During the last year only about 1,000 dollars were expended in the purchase of books, and during the present year a still smaller sum will be thus devoted. It has seemed to me my duty to state to you these facts, in order that you might understand the precise position of the Smithsonian Library, the ground of the expectations which had been raised respecting it, and the reasons why they had not been realized. I am happy to add to the statement which I have made, that whatever may have been the feeling with reference to the purchase of books, the "active operations" of the library department—the collection and publication of statistics of libraries, the increase and dissemination of bibliographical knowledge, the development and support of the catalogue system, &c.,—have met with cordial approval and support. This must be gratifying to those who hear me. I doubt not that whatever may be the policy of the Institution with reference to its own collections, it will do all that its means will allow for the benefit of other libraries.

For myself I have always believed, and still believe, that a large central library of reference and research will be collected at the Smithsonian Institution, if not by the expenditure of the funds of the Institution, by other means. The funds of the Institution are very small, in comparison with the necessities of literature and science in this country, and when we are obliged to choose among worthy objects, there will be sure to be different opinions. I feel, however, that the formation of the library is a matter sure to be accomplished—if not immediately, yet before many years. A great central library is an important national object; as necessary, to secure the literary independence of this people, as was the war of the Revolution to secure its political independence. It is an object which, besides attracting donations and bequests from the rich, may receive appropriations from our national treasury. Congress, having the control of the treasury of this rich, mighty, and intelligent nation, will not, I believe, be backward in making appropriations for this object, whenever it shall be suitably presented to them. Congress may be regarded as liberal in matters of science and of learning, whenever they are sure that the money will be honestly and properly expended. Many men do not believe this. But look at the action for replenishing the desolated hall of the Library of Congress. Most persons were of opinion that Congress could not be brought to make an appropriation exceeding $30,000 for this purpose ; but, when Mr. Chandler proposed $75,000, it was readily granted. It would have been had he asked $200,000, if they had thought that sum necessary, and believed that it would be honestly and judiciously devoted to the gathering of a good library.

There is one other remark I wish to make respecting the position of the Smithsonian Institution among the other literary institutions of the country. So far as I know, it possesses, claims, desires, no authority or power of dictation. The principle has been established and steadily pursued, of occupying, as far as possible, untenanted ground. The position of the Institution at Washington, its connection with the government, and its large fund, devoted by its donor and by the act of Congress to the promotion of the cause of knowledge, give to it the means of doing much which could not otherwise be accomplished for literature and science. In these efforts it needs and relies on the cordial support of other institutions, which, I am happy to say, it has always received. Whenever it is found that any other society or any individual is ready and able 'o take up and carry out its plans, they are immediately relinquished by us. I may here give one instance, that of Mr. Norton's *Literary Gazette*. Mr. Norton had formed the plan of publishing the Gazette, without knowing that a similar project had been recommended by myself for the bibliographical department of the Smithsonian Bulletin. He proposed to give the bibliographical intelligence in connection with advertisements, which he thought would eventually be profitable to him. When he saw what I had written, he came on to Washington, and offered to abandon his plan. But we were glad to find that he was willing to undertake to accomplish the same purpose which we had in view, and gave up the whole to him, offering him such assistance as we could render, and encouraging him to believe that the enterprise would prove a profitable one. I am happy to know that this expectation has been fully justified; and I hope that the prosperity of this useful journal will continually increase.

In reference to these remarks, Mr. HAYWARD, of Ohio, presented the following resolution, which was adopted unanimously.

Resolved, That the thanks of this Convention be presented to the Board of Regents and Officers of the Smithsonian Institution, for their steady and effective efforts for the increase and diffusion of knowledge among men, and particularly for the measures which they have adopted for the encouragement and promotion of the public libraries of our country; and we have great pleasure in looking to that institution as the central establishment of the United States for the furtherance of all such objects.

THE SMITHSONIAN CATALOGUE SYSTEM.

Prof. JEWETT then proceeded to remark:

The catalogue system of which I intend to speak, is one of those enterprises which could not have been carried into operation except under the protection and guidance of the Smithsonian Institution; nor can it be successful, unless it meets the hearty approval and co-operation of other libraries. I wish, therefore, to present the matter fully and explicitly to this Convention.

Few persons, except librarians, are aware of the nature and extent of the difficulties which have been encountered in attempting to furnish suitable printed catalogues of large and growing libraries; difficulties apparently insurmountable, and menacing a common abandonment of the hope of affording guides, so important, to the literary accumulation of the larger libraries of Europe.

While the catalogue of a large library is passing through the press, new books are received, the titles of which it is impossible, in the ordinary manner of printing, to incorporate with the body of the work. Recourse must then be had to a supplement. In no other way can the acquisitions of the library be made known to the public. If the number of supplements be multiplied, as they have been in the library of Congress, the student may be obliged to grope his weary way through ten catalogues, instead of one, in order to ascertain whether the book which he seeks be in the library. He cannot be certain, even then, that the book is not in the collection, for it may have been received since the last appendix was printed. Supplements soon become intolerable. The whole catalogue must then be re-arranged and re-printed. The expense of this process may be borne so long as the library is small, but it soon becomes burdensome, and, ere long, insupportable, even to national establishments.

There is but one course left—not to print at all. To this no scholar consents, except from necessity. But to this alternative, grievous as it is, nearly all the large libraries of Europe have been reluctantly driven.

More than a century has passed, since the printing of the catalogue of the Royal Library at Paris was commenced. It is not yet finished. No one feels in it the interest which he would, if he could hope to have its completeness sustained, when once brought up to a given date.

Not one European library, of the first class, has a complete printed catalogue, in a single work. The Bodleian Library is not an exception. It may be necessary to search six distinct catalogues, in order to ascertain whether any specified book was or was not in that collection, at the close of the year 1847.

This is, surely, a disheartening state of things. It has been felt and lamented by every one who has had the care of an increasing library.

As a remedy for this evil, it is proposed to stereotype the titles separately, and to preserve the plates or blocks, in alphabetical order of the titles, so as to be able readily to insert additional titles, in their proper places, and then to reprint the whole catalogue. By these means, the chief cost of republication (that of composition) together with the trouble of revision and correction of the press, would, except for new titles, be avoided. Some of the great difficulties which have so long oppressed and discouraged librarians, and involved libraries in enormous expenses, may be thus overcome.

The peculiar position of the Smithsonian Institution suggested the application of this plan, on a wider scale, and for a more important purpose, than that of merely facilitating the publication of new and complete editions of separate catalogues.

It had been proposed to form a general catalogue of all the books in the country, with reference to the libraries where each might be found. The plan of stereotyping titles separately, suggested the following system for the accomplishment of this important purpose:

1. The Smithsonian Institution to publish rules for the preparation of Catalogues.

2. Other institutions, intending to publish catalogues of their books, to be requested to prepare them in accordance with these rules, with a view to their being stereotyped under the direction of the Smithsonian Institution.

3. The Smithsonian Institution to pay the whole extra expense of stereotyping, or such part thereof as may be agreed upon.

4. The stereotyped titles to remain the property of the Smithsonian Institution.

5. Every library acceding to this plan, to have the right of using all the titles in the possession of the Institution as often as desired, for the printing of its own catalogue by the Smithsonian Institution, paying only the expense of making up the pages, of press-work, and of distributing the titles to their proper places.

6. The Smithsonian Institution to publish, as soon as possible, and at stated intervals, a General Catalogue of all Libraries coming into this system.

I have already presented to members of the Convention copies of an unfinished work entitled the "Smithsonian Catalogue System." It contains: 1. A detailed account of the system; 2. Rules for the preparation of Catalogues; 3. Examples illustrating the rules. As to the first two matters, the work is complete. It was intended to print as examples the titles of all the works, in the department of bibliography and literary history, in the Smithsonian Library. These titles, to the number of one thousand, are stereotyped and ready for use. The progress of the work was interrupted by the sickness and absence of two of the men on whom we relied. I have been able to print off a few copies, by using the type for the last form of the rules instead of the stereotype plates as in the rest of the book, by limiting the number of examples and omitting the indexes. I hope in a few weeks to be able to finish this book, and to present it through the Smithsonian Institution to the public, as the first detailed publication of the system. About three years ago I read a paper on the subject before the American Scientific Association. I did not present the matter before the public, till the practicability of stereotyping by separate titles had been demonstrated. Practical stereotypers had said that it could not be done. But the perseverance and ingenuity of a gentleman now present, the Rev. Mr. Hale, of Worcester, showed that it could be done by the electrotype process, and even by the common stereotype process. This point once proved, we sought the *best* method of executing the work. About this time, Mr. Josiah Warren, of Indiana, called our attention to the new process and material for stereotyping which he had patented. We gave them a thorough trial, and at last adopted them. We have done much to perfect the process, and we are now ready to show to experts in practical printing the results which we have attained. The perfecting of this mode of stereotyping, the adaptation of it to our purposes, and the arrangement of the practical details for the great work upon which we are commencing, have consumed much time and demanded great labor. The mechanical difficulties which we have had to meet and overcome will be appreciated by printers and stereotypers. The bibliographical difficulties will be fully understood by librarians. As soon as the practicability of the system had been established, as fully as it could possibly be, before its actual application on a large scale, and the value of it to the world of learning had been considered and proclaimed by a commission of the most competent men to whom the subject was referred by the Smithsonian Institution, the matter was presented to the Joint Library Committee of Congress. They considered it fully, and in the most liberal spirit, and finally recommended to Congress an appropriation for the cataloguing of its library upon this plan. This appropriation was readily granted. It is sufficient to enable us to prosecute the work till next December or January. It is not enough to finish the catalogue, but it is all that was asked for. We wish to proceed cautiously—demonstrating, step by step, the practicability and usefulness of our operations. The work on the catalogue of the Library of Congress is now in progress. The system is therefore in actual operation. . . . . . .

The title of every book and of each distinct edition is stereotyped upon a separate plate. The author's name also stands by itself. Each plate shows at a glance the heading to which it belongs. It is obvious that these plates may be placed together in alphabetical or other order, as may be desired. They are mounted on blocks for printing like other stereotype plates. The great ends to be gained are:

1. To avoid the necessity of preparing, composing, and correcting anew the titles once printed, when the Library has received accessions, or the alternative of printing the titles of these accessions in supplements, which are very inconvenient appendages.

2. To prevent the repetition of the work of preparation of titles, composition and correction of press, for copies of the same book in different libraries. The title once prepared and stereotyped, remains at the Smithsonian Institution, to be used by any Library having the same book.

3. To secure uniformity in the construction of catalogues, thus greatly facilitating the researches of the student.

It is obvious that the cost of the first catalogue will be greater than if it were not stereotyped. The work of preparation will also be more expensive. But the additional cost of the first edition will be more than saved in the first reprinting of the whole catalogue. It will be further understood that the sum paid by the first Library is not only for its own benefit, but for that of every other Library hereafter adopting the plan, so far as its books are the same. Congress is therefore now conferring a great boon upon other Libraries, while at the same time it is taking the course, in the end most economical, for the construction of the catalogues of its own Library. There will also be a great saving of the expense of paper and press-work under this system. It is customary now to print off a larger number of copies of every catalogue than are immediately wanted, because it cannot be known how many may be required before the catalogue can be reprinted. On this plan, when a new edition, with all additions incorporated can be had at any time, it will not be thought necessary to print more copies than enough to meet the immediate demand.

It should be mentioned as one of the most important advantages of this system, that it affords the means of attaining great accuracy in the catalogues. Every effort will be made to secure accuracy in the first instance. Librarians will not, however, be surprised to find numerous errors. This system offers the best means of detecting and correcting these errors. Every time that a title is used for a new catalogue, it must be very carefully compared with the book itself. Every mistake and variation will be reported in a friendly spirit, and immediately corrected. The catalogue will thus be constantly undergoing a process of verification and improvement.

Upon all these topics I have dwelt more fully and systematically in the pamphlet to which I have alluded. It may not be amiss for me to notice one or two objections which may occur to the minds of practical printers against the use of these stereotype plates. One is, that the plates, being used so often, will become worn, and that when new plates are inserted, the difference between the new and old plates will be observable on the printed sheets.

To this objection I can say in reply : First, the number of copies required for each catalogue would be so small that it would be many years before there would be any noticeable difference between the old and new plates, were they made from common type metal. But, secondly, the material which we employ is harder than type metal, and resists much longer the wear of the press. I presume that a run of 100,000 copies would not make any observable difference between the old plates and the new.

Another difficulty which may suggest itself to some, is in keeping the register and preserving a uniform length of pages. The register, so far as the top and sides of the page are concerned, can be kept most perfectly. Variations in the length of the pages cannot be entirely avoided. But if some pages be longer or shorter by three or four lines, it is not a very serious matter. It may offend a printer's eye, but would not be noticed by the general reader. I may remark, however, that there are several ways of reducing the inequalities. Very long titles may be stereotyped in two or three pieces. The titles on a short page may be spread apart, making the matter a little more open and thus elongating the page. The catalogue may be printed in double-column folio. This size is preferable for a catalogue on other accounts. It presents more titles to the eye at once, and it also saves paper.

I would not be understood as insisting upon the catalogue being in folio, nor, indeed, upon its being alphabetical. These are matters not essential to the system. Each librarian can choose for himself; the system possessing this great advantage, that it is equally applicable to the folio, quarto. or octavo size ; to alphabetical and to classed catalogues.

There is one other point which may be noticed. This kind of catalogue is not recommended for all purposes for which a catalogue or list of books may be desirable. It is proposed as the standard catalogue for reference in every library containing works of permanent value. It is proposed as the basis for all other apparatus, such as indexes, shelf-lists, "finding catalogues," or short title catalogues, which it may be thought that the peculiar circumstances of any library or every library require. From this catalogue all others may easily be made. This is supposed to be, in general, the first and most important of all the means for rendering a library serviceable to all classes of persons who may consult it.

With respect to the rules for preparing catalogues, it may be proper to make a few explanatory remarks. They were formed after a careful study of those adopted for the preparation of the catalogue of the British Museum. They were examined and discussed in detail by the catalogue commission appointed by the Smithsonian Institution. They have been carefully revised to meet exigencies which have occurred in the practical application of them. That they are perfect and all-sufficient, is not, indeed, to be supposed. On many points there would be a difference of opinion. An effort has been earnestly and honestly made to frame the best possible code. But whether it be absolutely the best or not, the great desideratum of uniformity will be attained by the adoption of it.

The practical operation of the rules has been considered, no less than the theoretical perfection of the catalogue. It is necessary to frame such rules as we may reasonably expect to be able to follow. I would gladly have required that the number of pages of every book (distinguishing those of prefatory and appended matter,) and the names of publishers should in all cases be given. But these would require much additional time and labor, and would considerably increase the bulk of the catalogue. It was thought best, therefore, to omit them. We must endeavor to make the catalogue accurate so far as it goes. The examination of the book should be thorough. Additional particulars may hereafter be added in the form of notes, without disturbing the work first done.

The work upon which we have entered is not the work of a day, nor of a year. It demands long-continued, patient labor. Should it be successful, as we have every reason to hope that it will be, its best results will be realized after we have ceased from our labors. But its immediate results will amply reward our efforts. Some of them are now almost attained. The catalogue of the Library of Congress will, it is hoped, be a valuable gift to the bibliographical world. To the list now nearly ready for publication, of the books in the department of bibliography and literary history, belonging to the Smithsonian Library, it will be easy to add those in other libraries not already catalogued. We can then present to librarians a complete catalogue of the bibliographical apparatus to be found in the country. Catalogues of books in other branches of knowledge are now in preparation. As we thus proceed from library to library, and from one department of learning to another, each work will be complete and useful in itself, while it constitutes a finished portion of the general catalogue.

At the conclusion of these remarks, Mr. Folsom presented the following resolutions :—

Resolved, That we have considered attentively the plan for constructing catalogues of libraries, and a general catalogue of the public libraries of the United States, by means of stereotype titles, proposed and developed by the Smithsonian Institution. That we regard it as an object of high importance to the interests of our public libraries, and to the promotion of learning, and worthy to share in the funds of the Institution, and the zealous exertions of its officers ; the more so as it is an enterprise which cannot be successfully prosecuted except under the protection, guidance and pecuniary support of this central establishment, for the increase and diffusion of knowledge.

Resolved, That we have learned with pleasure that Congress, on the recommendation of the Library Committee, made an appropriation for the practical testing of the plan in its application to the Library of Congress, and that the work is now in successful progress.

Resolved, That, as practical librarians and bibliographers, we take pride and satisfaction in the fact that a measure of so great literary utility has received the prompt and efficient support of our national legislature, and we would express the earnest hope that this support be extended to it liberally till its first great result, in the complete stereotyped catalogue of the Library of Congress, shall be attained.

Mr. Smith, of Philadelphia, said he had investigated Prof. Jewett's plan with considerable interest, and could heartily favor the resolutions. He thought the catalogue of the British Museum even might be completed, and thereby the scholars of the world be greatly benefited, by following this system. He thought the result of this experiment would be one grand catalogue of all the libraries of the United States.

Mr. Haven, of Worcester, said he thought the resolutions should contain some intimation that the idea was purely American in its inception and perfection.

Mr. Folsom said the intent of the resolutions was to stamp it as American.

The propriety of stating more clearly the fact, that the invention of separate stereotyped titles was purely American, was advocated by Mr. Haven, Prof. Greene, and others.

Prof. JEWETT said that within the last few months he had heard that a claim for this invention had been set up in France, by the Chevalier de La Garde, an employee of the National Library. After the speech he

[Mr. J.] delivered before the American Scientific Association, M. de la Garde published a letter in the *Moniteur*, in which he stated that he had formed a similar plan eighteen years previous, that he had published an account of it in 1845, and that he had endeavored to secure its adoption. The plan of the Chevalier de la Garde differed in many respects from his own, but still it contained the idea of separate stereotype titles. Mr. J. stated still further, that this claim was entirely unknown to him until long after he had fully matured and had proposed his own system. He had never heard of such a proposition from any source, till after he had suggested it. He certainly hoped that full justice would be done to any earlier efforts than his own which may have been made in this direction.

Mr. HAVEN remarked, that in every great discovery there was always found a number of men who laid claim to be the originators, but it was universally admitted that he who carried a discovery to its successful application was the one entitled to the credit as inventor.

Mr. FOLSOM said that the same idea had struck him thirty years ago, and therefore he had a better claim than the French gentleman. Neither claim amounted to anything. The idea had produced nothing practical and useful. He would say, however, that though he had had the idea, when Prof. Jewett mentioned it to him he said that its practical development was "impossible."

Mr. GUILD, of Providence, said he had at first entertained serious doubts as to the practicability of the system. Those doubts were now entirely removed, and he hoped the time would soon come when every library in the land would have its catalogue made out by means of separate stereotyped titles.

The first resolution was then amended as follows:

Resolved, That we have considered attentively the plan for constructing catalogues of libraries, and a general catalogue of the public libraries of the United States, by means of separate stereotype titles, *originated and proposed by Prof. C. C. Jewett*, and developed by *him while librarian of* the Smithsonian Institution, etc.

The three resolutions, as thus amended, were then unanimously adopted.

Mr. VINTON, of St. Louis, then presented the following:

Resolved, That a Committee of three be appointed by this Convention, to prepare a history of the invention of applying movable stereotype plates to the printing of the separate titles in a catalogue; and that their report be embodied in a written memorial, to be presented at the next annual session of this Convention, in order that it may be printed at the expense of the Convention.

The resolution was carried unanimously—and Mr. Folsom, of Boston, Mr. Guild, of Providence, and Rev. Mr. Hale, of Worcester, were appointed that Committee.

CENTRAL NATIONAL LIBRARY.

Mr. FOLSOM offered the following resolutions, which were adopted unanimously :

Resolved, That the establishment of a great central library for reference and research, while it is demanded by the condition of the United States as to general civilization and intellectual advancement, is especially interesting to this Convention from the bearing it would have upon libraries throughout the country.

Resolved, That we deem such an establishment as being eminently worthy of support from the national treasury, and that in no way can the government better promote the progress of learning through the whole country, than by placing a central national library under the administration of the Smithsonian Institution.

POPULAR LIBRARIES.

The importance of popular libraries in every part of our country, was introduced by Rev. S. OSGOOD, of New York, in the following remarks :

I suppose, Mr. President, that no business is at present formally before the Convention, and that it is in order now for any member to suggest topics of interest for the consideration of the Committee just chosen. I hardly feel entitled to speak at this early stage of the proceedings, yet there may be something in my position, as a delegate and not a librarian, which will allow me to speak of your valuable profession, as one of yourselves, which you, with your characteristic professional modesty, could not do.   When I first saw the call for this Convention in the newspapers, the idea struck me as a capital one, especially from its probable influence upon the public spirit of the country, as well as upon the fellow-feeling of librarians as a professional class.   I little expected, however, to take any part in your proceedings, until being surprised by an appointment from the Providence Athenæum to represent its interests here, and thus renew with that noble institution a relation so much valued years ago.   It is proper, therefore, for me to make some suggestions touching the welfare of our popular class of libraries, as representing an institution so prominent among them, and already numbering nearly twenty thousand volumes of the choicest books within its possession.

May I not, however, say a word of congratulation at the appearance of things thus far in your assembly.   It is good to be here with so large a class of men, so useful and laborious in one of the most important callings on earth—the keepers and the choosers of the aliment that nurtures the mental life of the nation.   Every man is better for honoring his vocation, and I hope that it will be one of the results of your deliberations to make you think more highly of your work, and to bring to its labors a more cordial *esprit du corps*. The profession to which I belong owes an especial debt of gratitude to yours, so dependent are we, in all our more advanced states, upon the treasures of which you are the custodians. I surely never felt more disposed to acknowledge the obligation than now when addressing a chair occupied by one who has done such eminent service to the library cause in this country. Some ten years since how we rejoiced in your return to the city of Providence, from your European tour, backed by a force of some ten thousand volumes of the choicest ancient and modern literature, to double the library of Brown University, and to multiply the resources of many earnest scholars, more abounding in the spirit than in the apparatus of liberal study. Much is said of the power of foreign immigration, and often the most startling statistics disclose the new elements of hope and peril that are landed every year upon our shores. Such immigration as you have promoted is all hopeful, and in nothing perilous. A blessing upon such arrivals of thousands of authors embodied in their books, and not a single shabby fellow among them all. What a great subject this matter of selecting and diffusing of books opens upon us! How much light would be thrown upon the inner life of the nation, if we could only trace the influence of good books as they make their noiseless progress throughout the land, spreading so much light, quickening so much energy, checking so much, and beguiling so much pain and sorrow! Honor to this movement that aims to help on the good cause. Too many bad books make their stealthy advances, that need to be tracked to their dens, even as the pestilence that walketh in darkness needs to be hunted to its hiding-place. Honor to every man who circulates two good books where only one circulated before. Remember Milton's noble words:—" As good almost kill a man as kill a good book: who kills a man, kills a reasonable creature—God's image; but he who destroys a good book, kills reason itself, kills the image of God as it were in the eye."

I should be very glad at the fitting time to say my poor word in behalf of the highest class of public libraries, and of the need of bringing them up to a more adequate standard. Proud as we are of our four or five great libraries, there is not one of them, not even that of Harvard University, my own cherished Alma Mater, that affords the requisite means for the thorough study of any one topic of recondite learning, even, if of practical science. Any scholar who tries to investigate any ancient or historical subject will find, to his regret, that no library in the country has a plummet that can sound its depths. What facilities the noble Astor Library may afford, we can judge better when its merits are known and its treasures are consolidated.

There is no reason for being down-hearted at this state of things, for we cannot expect soon to rival the great libraries of Europe, and our present task is rather with the increase and improvement of libraries for the people, than with great central institutions such as the wealth of centuries only can endow. As the mass of the people obtain a higher culture by means at hand in every town and city, the demand for the highest class of books will increase, and the hope of national collections will brighten. Now, what shall prevent our America from leading all nations of the earth *longo intervallo* in the number and value of our popular Institutes and Athenæums? We are probably not much behind, if at all behind, any portion of Europe in the number of books collected in our villages, and available to the community at large. But not a tithe of the progress has been made that should have been made. What prevents every community of a thousand inhabitants from having its well-chosen library of a thousand volumes? and if this ratio were to be carried out in all our towns, how vast would be the increase and how noble the triumph of a sound popular literature! May not this Convention do something, by its discussions and action, to call attention to this matter, and rouse many a slumbering township to its imperative duty? Who shall presume to estimate adequately the advantages coming from the establishment of a good library in a community not before so favored? The immediate vicinity and the whole nation share in the benefit.

Many a thriving town needs some such centre of generous and elevating interest as an attractive library must be, and it should be considered but half civilized until such a centre is established. It should be one of the first things to be pointed out to the traveler in new regions. When in distant places, we yearn for some familiar objects, and we feel at once at home when we hear the pleasant church bells, and see the goodly company of stout men, fair women and sprightly children on their way to the sanctuary. How this home-feeling is deepened when we enter some neat and well-filled library, and look upon the array of good authors open to the perusal of the people, and feel a new sense even of humane and religious fellowship, as we, think of the grand intellectual catholicity that unites the whole civilized world in the same literary allegiance. The village library attracts to itself every congenial ally, and tends to diffuse social refinement as well as intellectual light. The Lyceum, often suggested by the tastes formed by reading, repays the debt by popular lectures, whose proceeds often pay the expense of new books, and there is no more cheering view of our Young America than that afforded by the thousands and tens of thousands of young men, of generous and inquiring minds, who gather around the popular institute, with its library and courses of lectures.

This Convention will not meet in vain, if it shall give the incentive to form one new institution of the kind anywhere in the land. Every such library tends to foster a worthy public spirit among citizens of ample means. Many a successful merchant of the city, who has thriven largely in some "sugar trade or cotton line," and who abounds far more in generous impulses than literary attainments, would rejoice to send to his native town or village some choice work of art, or valuable selection of books, as a token of kindly remembrance, if an institution existed that should suggest the hint and indicate the method to the benefactor. It will be found that every well organized popular library has been much enriched by such donations, none more so than that which I now represent, that Athenæum so nobly endowed by the heirs of Ives, so strengthened by the bequest of Butler, and favored every year by the generosity of men less abounding in wealth, yet not less wanting in the right spirit.

The whole country grows by such institutions, for they at once collect the local and fugitive literature, so important to the natural history, and they create a demand for the best class of books, securing of themselves an encouraging market for a good sized edition of every work of undoubted value. I call your attention seriously to the value of such enterprises, and urge you to do something to extend and improve them. Following the report prepared by yourself, Mr. President, under the auspices of Congress, I find the number of libraries, of a public character, containing 1,000 volumes and upwards, to be only 423, and the aggregate number of volumes in the 694 libraries reported, exclusive of school libraries, to be 2,201,623. Now, sir, where is the town of any importance that should not at once have its thousand of good books circulating among its people, and what but the want of the true spirit shall prevent our two millions of volumes from swelling to twenty millions, nay, reaching before the year of the next census the full limit of our numerical population, although it may exceed thirty millions? Sir, with your leave, I offer the following resolutions:

Resolved, That while we maintain most decidedly the importance of libraries of the highest class, in furtherance of the most advanced literary and scientific studies, and rejoice in the rise and progress of our few great collections of books for professional scholars, we are convinced that for the present our chief hope must be in the establishment and improvement of *popular* libraries throughout the land.

Resolved, That the Business Committee be requested to call attention to the desirableness of a popular Library Manual, which shall embody the most important information upon the chief points in question, especially upon—

1. The best organization of a Library society, in regard to its officers, laws, funds, and general regulations.

2. The best plans for Library edifices, and the arrangements of the shelves and books, with the requisite architectural drawings.

3. The most approved method of making out and printing catalogues.

4. The most desirable principle to be followed in the selection and purchase of books, as to authors and editions ; with lists of such works as are best suited for libraries of various sizes, from 500 to 1,000 volumes or upwards.

Resolved, That the Business Committee be requested to consider the expediency of memorializing Congress to procure the preparation of such a Manual, through the agency of the Smithsonian Institution.

These resolutions were referred to the following committee, who are to take action upon them and report at the next meeting of the Convention; viz.: Rev. S. Osgood, Prof. C. C. Jewett, and Mr. R. A. Guild.

Subsequently, Rev. GORHAM D. ABBOTT presented the following resolutions :—

Resolved, That the time has now arrived when the extension of well-selected public libraries, of 1,000, 5,000 and 10,000 volumes, throughout the towns and villages, the associations, the institutions, the schools of every kind in the United States, has become a matter of the greatest importance to the future welfare of our country.

Resolved, That a committee of three be appointed to report a digested plan for the promotion of this object at the next meeting of this Convention.

Mr. HALE seconded these resolutions, and hoped that some means might be found to carry out the principle. But he called the attention of his friend who moved it to the danger which lurked in every such plan ; that, so soon as such a list of books was suggested, there started up a bookseller's job, and the benefit of the list was lost in the struggles of those who sought to be the only publishers who could supply the libraries. The School Boards of the various States have found this difficulty so incurable, that they have refrained from suggesting any list of school books as an official list to be followed. There was, too, always, in every town, some peculiar want to be satisfied, which no general list could meet.

He took the opportunity presented in this resolution, to attempt some definition as to the real character of a "popular library :" the words had been frequently used in the sessions of the Convention, but needed more accuracy in their use than, out of the Convention, they always gained. In fact, there were two distinct meanings of the word "popular," and it is to one of these only that the resolution of his friend referred, or his support of it. That is "popular" which at the moment is attractive, as the play bills in the streets said Miss Julia Dean was a "popular" actress. That is "popular" in another sense, which is of real use to the whole people ; and it is in this sense only that the resolution contemplates a popular library.

The great duty and the great difficulty of the trustees of popular libraries is, to keep them true to this last sort of popularity, and to turn as sternly as possible from the temptation to buy books which are popular, only because at the moment attractive, for this last class of purchases becomes the most costly possible. In a few years, in a few months even, such books lose all their attraction, and the library has bought them at the highest price, to give them shelf-room afterwards, when they are worth really nothing at all. A circulating library sold at auction, is a good index of the worth, after a few years, of books "popular" in their day. Mr. H. illustrated this view of the change of value of books by one or two instances.

He then said, that the enterprise of the princely publishers of this city had relieved library purchasers of a great part of the difficulty in balancing the two "popularities." That magnificent enterprise which

157

has made books cheaper in America than in any country in the world, makes it so easy for every man to get hold of the cheap literature which is simply transitory in its character, that there is really no need now to accumulate that in a public library. At the same time, this very cheap literature, which, with all its dangers, and they are great, was still the greatest blessing to the training of this country, had created, and would still create, the popular appetite for books behind it, which the public library, if it was really popular, ought to supply. The youngster who had bought for a shilling the fascinating account of the Russian Campaign, by Alexandre Dumas, has a right to find in the public library the more fascinating pages of the Count Segur, from which it is drawn. To-day, said Mr. Hale, the great literary question seems likely to be, whether Napoleon was the best, greatest, and most religious of men, or the worst, meanest, and least religious of men. Now, the young men and young women who are interested in that discussion, have a right to claim of a popular library, that when they turn from Mr. Abbott's fascinating life of him in *Harper*, they shall find the only reading about him, which is more fascinating, in the details of his own dispatches, or the memoirs of his own generals. For the popular life which circulates a thousand copies in every large town, they need not look to the public library : for the materials to which it refers them they must look there ; and they have a right to claim that they shall be found there. And this merit has the purchase of such books, that every year their value increases, while every year the value of books, which are simply the talk of the day, falls off till they are worth nothing at all.

The resolutions were adopted, and Messrs. Haven, of Worcester, Abbott, of New York, and Jewett, of Washington, appointed as the committee for reporting a plan at the next annual meeting.

DISTRIBUTION OF PUBLIC DOCUMENTS.

Mr. LLOYD P. SMITH, of Philadelphia, presented the following resolutions :—

Whereas, The documents published by order of the Congress of the United States, are printed in large numbers at the public expense, and

Whereas, It is desirable that they should be so distributed as to be accessible for reference to all citizens, and at the same time preserved for posterity, therefore,

Resolved, That a Committee of two be appointed to memorialize Congress, on behalf of this Convention, requesting the passage of a joint resolution, granting to the Smithsonian Institution, for distribution among the principal Public Libraries throughout the United States, copies of all such Journals of Congress, Senate Documents, House Documents, Reports of Committees, and other State Papers as may hereafter be printed by order of Congress.

Mr. SMITH said it was unnecessary, with such an intelligent audience as that before him, to expatiate on the importance of the Public Docu ments and State Papers of the United States. They were constantly wanted for reference, not only by historians, but by lawyers, claimants on the Government, and citizens generally, seeking information. In a word, they are invaluable.

He would rather say a few words on the right which he conceived the Convention had, in its representative character, to call upon Congress so to distribute the Public Documents that they may be forever accessible to their constituents. These documents are printed at vast expense, which comes out of the pockets of the citizens generally. By the present mode of distribution to members of Congress and a few favored libraries only, they become, soon after publication, so scarce as to be practically useless, whereas, by the proposed distribution to the public libraries of the country, and for purposes of reference, (he presumed every library there represented was accessible to all civil gentlemen,) they would always be at hand for the use of those for whose benefit they were, in fact, printed. The Convention did not, therefore, by passing these resolutions, come before Congress in the attitude of beggars, but rather as demanding, respectfully but firmly, for the people at large, their own.

Not that he would imply that there was, on the part of Congress, the slightest indisposition to do what in it lay for the " increase and diffusion of knowledge." On the contrary, the facts just mentioned by the Librarian of the Smithsonian Institution, not to speak of the munificient appropriation of something like $150,000 for a work which, it was supposed, would be a history of the Indian Tribes, showed that Congress was not indifferent to the claims of learning. But there was a natural and proper dread of jobbery and corruption in making these appropriations. In the case just mentioned the money had better have been thrown into the Potomac than that the Government should be disgraced. How much better had the $150,000 been spent in building up, on the foundation of the Congress Library, or that of the Smithsonian Institution, a great National Library, which should be for this country what the British Museum, the Bibliothèque du Roi, the Royal Library of Berlin, and other national institutions are for the scholars of the old world. And this led him to speak of the plan of distribution which, by these resolutions, was recommended to the wisdom of Congress. If a list of libraries was recommended by this Convention to the favor of Congress, those Senators and Representatives whose constituents were not included, would either oppose the resolutions, or, by adding amendment after amendment, endanger their passage; or if they should be passed, no provision would be made for libraries hereafter to be founded. No objection, he thought, could be made in any quarter, to handing over, every session, say at least 300 copies of all Public Documents to the Regents of the Smithsonian Institution, to be, at their discretion, distributed to such libraries as would be likely to use them for the greatest benefit of the country.

Mr. HALE was very glad to see this subject brought up. He looked upon it as the most important subject that could be brought before them. The government of the United States did more for the encouragement of Literature than any government of the world, but still, through some mistake at Washington, the documents printed at the public expense were not circulated as generally as they ought to be. A complete collection of all the public documents of the United States could not now be found anywhere.

The above resolutions were unanimously adopted. Messrs. Smith, of Philadelphia, and Folsom, of Boston, were appointed the Committee. The president also was subsequently added.

Mr. WALLACE, of Philadelphia, offered the following resolutions, which he introduced with a few appropriate remarks. The resolutions were unanimously passed:—

Resolved, As the sense of this Convention, that the completeness of public law libraries throughout the country, and the interest of American jurisprudence, would be promoted by having, in each incorporated or public law library of the United States, a complete set of the *Statutes at large* of every State of the Union, in their original and unabridged condition. And that, as these volumes appear only from year to year, as they are not often on sale by law booksellers, nor easily procured from year to year by application, therefore, that this Convention respectfully suggests to the Governors, Secretaries of State, Legislatures or other public authorities having power to distribute these volumes, to make some permanent orders for transmitting to the Smithsonian Institution, at Washington, for distribution to the library of the Law Association at Philadelphia, and to the other public or incorporated law libraries throughout the United States, a certain number of copies of their statute laws, as published from year to year by the Legislatures of the respective States, in the original and unabridged condition.

Resolved, That the Secretary of the Law Association of Philadelphia, be requested, with leave of that body, to transmit a copy of this resolution to the respective Governors and Secretaries of State throughout the Union, with any remarks he may see proper to make on the subject.

The following, which was presented by Mr. GUILD, was also adopted:

Resolved, That the members of this Convention cordially recommend the mutual interchange, so far as may be practicable, of the printed catalogues of all our public libraries.

INDEXES TO AMERICAN LITERATURE.

1.

Mr. EDWIN WILLIAMS presented the following plan for an Index to American Newspapers:

Proposed Index of American Newspapers, and Chronology of Important Events for the last 125 years.

The undersigned, as a member of the New York Historical Society, brought before one of the regular meetings of that institution a proposal, for causing to be made an index of the principal American newspapers on their files, extending over a period of one hundred and twenty-five years, in so many serial volumes. The proposal was favorably received by the Society, and referred to a special committee, of which the undersigned is chairman, with power to carry the same into effect; and he desires an expression of the opinion of this Convention on the subject, believing that it is important to the interests of Historical Literature, as it must open new sources of information, particularly to those engaged in researches either for literary or business purposes.

The plan proposes an index and chronological arrangement of the most important matters relative to American history, which may be found in the newspapers in the library of the Historical Society, principally those published in the city of New York, commencing in or about the year 1728, and continued to the present year; the index to include also the volumes of the *National Intelligencer*, which has been published at the city of Washington for the last half century. It might also embrace the volumes of *Niles's Register*, published in Baltimore, from 1811 to 1849, to which there is a semi-annual but no general index, except for the first twelve volumes.

The proposed index would probably comprise two octavo volumes of about one thousand pages, arranged on the plan of Holmes' American Annals, which comprise two volumes of chronology, from 1492 to 1826. Five or more persons could be employed in the work of preparing the index, under the auspices of the committee of the New York Historical Society, and the time required need not exceed two years. The Society would then publish the work in two volumes, in an edition of one thousand or one thousand five hundred copies. The total expense is estimated at ten thousand dollars; one half for the preparation, and one half for printing and binding.

To provide for the payment of the expense, it is proposed to obtain two hundred subscribers, at fifty dollars each, and the volumes, when published, to belong to the subscribers, each receiving five copies of the work for his share of fifty dollars.

EDWIN WILLIAMS.

Mr. HAVEN presented the following resolution in relation to this subject, which was adopted.

Resolved, That this Convention approve of the plan of the proposed index and chronology of American newspapers, belonging to the New York Historical Society, on the plan submitted by Edwin Williams, and referred, for the purpose of being carried out, to a special committee of that Society, and that we recommend the proposition to the favorable consideration and support of the friends of literature throughout the United States, particularly to libraries and other literary institutions.

2.

A copy of a new index to the Periodical Literature of England and America was exhibited to the Convention, and, on motion of Mr. Folsom, it was unanimously

Resolved, That we have examined the work entitled "Index to Periodicals," by W. F. Poole, Librarian of the Mercantile Library of Boston, and that we approve of its plan and execution, and we recommend that a similar system of indexing be extended to the transactions and memoirs of learned societies.

3.

The following plan for a Catalogue of Standard Works relating to America was presented by Mr. DISTURNELL, and referred to the Business Committee.

STANDARD WORKS ON AMERICA, showing its History, Geography, and Statistics.

Also, a *Catalogue of Works* relating to *American History, Geography, and Statistics* of Population, Emigration, Agriculture, Commerce, Manufactures, Internal Improvements, Minerals, Coinage, and Banking.

The *Historical and Geographical Works*, including Maps and Charts, to date from the first discovery of America, by Columbus, to the present time. The *Statistical Works* to date from the first enumeration of the population of the United States, in 1790 or 1800, to the present period. "*Statistics*," although of modern date, the subject having first been brought forward and matured by Sir John Sinclair, of Scotland, during the last half and first part of the present century, is no doubt destined to become one of the most important sciences for the advancement of the human race. Enough is already known, from official and reliable statements, to form correct conclusions in regard to the working of different systems, whether relating to governments or domestic relations. Everything that can be numbered, weighed, or measured can be made the subject of minute inquiry and careful registry. What were formerly considered pure accidents, and so exempt from close examination, or beneath notice, have been shown, under the statistician's arrangement, to be the products of general laws, and to have a real and systematic bearing upon the welfare of man.

As the *Science of Statistics* is of so recent date, it is necessary to unite History and Geography in order to make the chain of knowledge perfect from the first discovery of the American continent, or its islands, in 1492, to the present period.

A complete list of *Standard Works* on information relating to the above kindred subjects, with the date of first publication, whether in bound volumes, manuscripts, public documents, pamphlets, or separate articles in magazines, &c., giving the names of compilers and authorities as far as possible, would afford great assistance to the seeker after *useful knowledge*, aid in the formation of private and public libraries, and thus be a lasting benefit to the present and future generations.

CLASSIFICATION OF WORKS INTO CATALOGUES.

1.

The following letter from M. Merlin, of Paris. was presented to the Convention by Mr. C. B. Norton :—

PARIS, 29th August, 1853.

DEAR SIR :—In promising to send to your Convention a slight bibliographical offering, I feel that I have not consulted my strength nor my time, and I must beg you to judge indulgently of these pages, traced in haste, and with the sole desire of expressing to you, as well as to the learned gentlemen who will assemble, my sympathy with their efforts.

I am happy to learn that one of the questions likely to be proposed at your bibliographical meeting is, the choice of some plan of classification proper to be adopted by the Libraries of the United States. Having been long impressed with the insufficiency of the different methods in use or proposed, I have made this important question the object of my study, and I have in press, at the Imperial Printing Office, a work in which, after having reviewed, analyzed, and estimated all that has been done up to the present time, especially in France, I now propose a new method, and give you herewith its principal points. I have already made use of this system of classification in several catalogues. That of the rich library of the celebrated Orientalist, Sylvestre de Sacy, edited by me, in 3 vols. 8vo., Paris, 1843 to 1847, shows the application of my system, and has some explanations in the preface.

In my opinion every systematic bibliographical classification should be based upon the logical classification of the sciences. I have therefore sought, in the first place, for the most natural order of arranging the different branches of human knowledge, independently of all application to bibliography, and it is from that order that I have deduced my bibliographical system.

It is very difficult, I am aware, to judge correctly of a system from these detached portions. Nevertheless, I do not hesitate to transcribe for you some passages from my forthcoming work, which I think will give you an insight into my plan. If there are any obscure or doubtful passages, I trust that they will be explained by the work itself on its appearance.

"According to my views, a system of bibliographical classification is a logical chain of great classes and their subdivisions, whose formation and order are the result of a few principles, which serve as a base to the system. The great object of bibliographical classification is to assist the memory, by presenting information which will facilitate the inquirer in his search after books that he already knows to exist, and impart to him

4*

information concerning those with which he is unacquainted. This is almost the same as presenting the literary history of each science in a synoptical form. This result can only be attained by bringing together all the works that treat on the same subject, and by arranging them in such order that the mind shall pass naturally from each subject to that which should follow or precede it; and in this way the place where any subject is found will be a sort of definition of its nature, and its distinctive characteristics. . . . . It is from this double operation, that is to say, from the bringing together similar subjects in their special groups, and determining the order which should be given to these groups, that their logical connection will be made manifest, and great assistance be given to the memory and mind. . .

"But in order that this logical connection shall really assist the memory and the mind, it must be easy to comprehend and bear in mind the principles according to which the subjects have been brought together, and their order determined. . . .

"If principles are adopted from merely abstract considerations, the classification will fail of accomplishing its end; it will be intelligible only to the minds of the few, and the best memory will fail to retain it. . . .

"If, on the contrary, the divisions are taken from the nature of the objects to be classified, and their order is based upon those great laws of nature which may be daily noted, the system will become intelligible to all, and every one's memory will be assisted.

General Classification of the Sciences, independent of Bibliography.

"Heretofore the Sciences have been generally classified according to arbitrary or metaphysical considerations, so that the progress of the Sciences, their comparative value, the relation which they bear to each other, their various applications, the nature of the moral faculties, the sources of human knowledge. . . .

"Throwing aside these abstract considerations, I would rest upon principles which I consider less subject to discussion and more easy to be understood. . . .

"According to my view, the first elements of scientific classification should be taken from the subjects treated. Compare the Sciences with each other, and you will not fail to see that the most certain and the most unchangeable characteristic which distinguishes one from the other is the subject itself, and their position is, therefore, to be decided upon according to the nature of the subject treated. It is from this subject that they almost always take their name; but the same subject may be considered under different views, and may thus give rise to several Sciences connected with each other by the identity of the subject, but distinct according to the point of view from which each is considered. . .

"Thence result two principal and distinct things to be considered; first, the general subject, which will serve to separate these Sciences into groups; second, the point of view which will distinguish the Sciences of each group from one another. . . .

" The subject has first given us the distinctive character, according to which our divisions will be formed ; it will also give us the order of these divisions. Since each group of Sciences represents a special subject, it is evident that the order of these groups should be modeled from the subjects which they represent. . . .

" Notwithstanding the indefinite variety of the subjects of human knowledge, all are material things, or are connected with material things by ties more or less direct, more or less intimate. If, then, we can find the most natural order for the productions of Creation, we shall have found the most natural order for the subjects of human knowledge, and, consequently, for human knowledge itself. . . . . . . It is not difficult to discover this order; it is seen by us at all times; it is that which the Creator himself has traced in his works, by graduating with such admirable regularity the organization of all beings, from the stone up to man.

" I would accordingly classify human knowledge by the objects of which it treats, either directly or indirectly, all arranged in the organic scale of being, and graduate this scale according to the chronological order of creation; that is to say, rising from the most simple to the most perfect.

" As to the subjects which treat of intellectual abstractions, of the moral world, or considerations of the social state, we shall see, by what follows, how they take their place in the outline that I have just traced.

" I will proceed by analysis, showing the whole before the sections, the entire plan before the details, things in general before those in particular.

Great Divisions.

" In the universality of being we see, as a first division, on one side the Creator, on the other the Creation. All the ideas that relate to God, to whatever opinion or religion they may belong, will form a principal group, that I shall designate by the title of THEOLOGICAL SCIENCES.

" The Sciences and the Arts which treat of the whole or any portion of those myriads of created beings, shall be comprised under the common title of COSMOLOGICAL SCIENCES.

" Since cause is before effect, the science which treats of God should be before all other sciences, and it would be so in my classification, without the principles of analytical exposition by which my system is arranged, and according to which every science which embraces several objects ought to precede that which treats only of those objects. Now Theology has only God for its object, and there is another science which treats of God and the Creation, that is, PHILOSOPHY; not Psychology, which only describes the human soul, not Moral Philosophy, which lays lays down rules for social life, but Philosophy, as known to the Ancients, treating of first causes, of the Essence of Being, of the Creator and created things; in a word, embracing everything in an encyclopedic manner; Philosophy will then precede Theology, and after it will come the Sciences which relate to created things.

From this order spring three great divisions,

I. PHILOSOPHY,
II. THEOLOGICAL SCIENCES.
III. COSMOLOGICAL SCIENCES.

The division of Cosmological Sciences will furnish the following groups:

1. MATHEMATICAL SCIENCE.
2. PHYSICAL   "
3. ASTRONOMICAL   "
4. GEOLOGICAL   "
5. MINERALOGICAL   "
6. PHYTOLOGICAL   "
7. ZOOLOGICAL   "
8. ANTHROPOLOGICAL   "

As to the sciences which relate to Man, their division and order are not less simple or less natural. I consider Man under two heads, Individual Man and Man in Society. Individual Man presents me with two divisions, Physical Man and Moral Man. Society also furnishes us with two divisions, the Social or Political Sciences and the Historical Sciences.

This is, sir, the outline of my classification of the Sciences without the Bibliographical application. This application changes nothing of importance, it only adds numerous subdivisions and another class, POLYGRAPHY.

I should be very much honored if my method were judged by your learned librarians worthy of being applied to the literary collections which are made all over America. But, whatever may be the judgment passed upon it, I shall be always delighted, sir, with the circumstance which has procured for me the opportunity of making your acquaintance, and to prove to you the great respect with which I am, sir,

Your very devoted servant,

R. MERLIN.

Mr. CHARLES B. NORTON.

2.

A Paper on the Classified Index of the Catalogue of the Philadelphia Library Company, prepared for the Librarians' Convention, by LLOYD P. SMITH, ESQ.

GENTLEMEN:—It has occurred to me that a short account of the manner of arranging and cataloguing the books of the Library Company of Philadelphia, might give rise to a discussion on those subjects which would be mutually instructive.

The Philadelphia Library has been in existence 121 years, and now numbers 65,000 vols. The books are arranged on the shelves according to a plan perhaps somewhat peculiar; that is, simply according to size. There are four sets of numbers, viz.: of folios, quartos, octavos, and duodecimos. This plan has some advantages as well as some disadvantages. It gives a neat and uniform appearance to the books as they stand on the shelves, and it makes it easy to ascertain at once whether a book is "in" or not. There is one exact spot where each volume ought to be; if it is not there it must be "out." It has the disadvantage that the works on the same subject are not together. This is, however, less important with us than in those libraries where the cases are open to the publi cor to members for inspection. The books in the Philadelphia Library are always kept under lock and key, the titles on the backs being, however, visible through the wires which protect them. When a book is wanted, the catalogue indicates the number and size, and, on the principle of "a place for everything and everything in its place," it is readily found.

It is obvious that, in our system, this strict dependence (where the librarian's memory is at fault) on the Catalogue makes a good one of the greatest importance.

When I took charge of the Library, in Jan., 1849, the state of the Catalogues was this:—

All the books acquired by the Library before 1835 were included in one general Catalogue in two volumes. Those added from 1835 to 1844 were embraced in the First Supplement, and those from 1844 to 1849 in the Second Supplement.

The great Catalogue of 1835 was arranged, according to subjects, into the usual five grand divisions of Religion, Jurisprudence, Sciences and Arts, Belles Lettres, and History. These chief heads were subdivided with considerable minuteness, each subdivision being arranged alphabetically by authors' names, and anonymous books being placed at the end. Of the remarkable accuracy and judgment (indicating extensive acquirements in the compiler) with which the titles of books are classified in this Catalogue, I cannot forbear speaking. It is the work of George Campbell, Esq., from 1806 to 1829 the Librarian of the Institution, and still, I am happy to say, its Secretary.

"Thank God for the makers of dictionaries!" a pious Oxford student was overheard to ejaculate; and I think, gentlemen, those who use the collections under our care have reason to be equally grateful that there are such persons as the makers of catalogues.

But, however admirable may be the arrangement of a Systematic Catalogue, it constantly happens that those who use it are at a loss under what head to look for a particular work. An alphabetical Index, therefore, especially of authors' names, becomes necessary; and such an Index, but partial and so incomplete as not to be depended on, was extemporised as the Catalogue of 1835, was going through the press, and added to it as an Appendix. The Supplements of 1844 and 1849 are totally destitute of such an Index. To make sure that a book is not in the Philadelphia Library, it is necessary, therefore, to look through three Catalogues; and if, as constantly happens, it is doubtful under what head a book would fall, or, again, if the title of a book is known, but not the author's name, the search is a very tedious one, and sometimes hopeless.

To remedy these evils, I conceived the following plan, viz.: to consolidate the two Supplements, together with the MS. list of works added since 1849, into one Catalogue, classified like that of 1835, and to be called vol. 3, the paging to run on continuously from vol. 2, which itself follows that of vol. 1. It is not proposed to consolidate the whole into one complete Catalogue, on account of the expense, which would be about $5,000. But most of the advantages of such a consolidation, together with some others not attainable by that process, will be secured by an alphabetical INDEX to the whole, on which I have been now more than two years engaged.

In making this Index the plan is, to take for a basis the present imperfect Index to the Catalogue of 1835, and going over each title again in that Catalogue,

I. To examine whether the author's name (if any) is already indexed, and, if not, to index it on a slip of paper, adding a short title of the book and the page of the Catalogue on which it is to be found.

II. To index the translators' and annotators' names.

III. To take the most important word or words of the title, and index it by them, as well as, in some cases, by some other word more likely to be referred to as the subject.

It will sometimes happen, therefore, that, on this plan, a book will be indexed five or six times, or even more : *e. g.*, "6,411, O. The Spy Unmasked; or, Memoirs of Enoch Crosby, alias Harvey Birch, comprising many interesting anecdotes never before published. By H. L. Barnum. New York, 1828."

This work (like *all* biography, poetry, and sermons) is not at present indexed at all. By the plan proposed it will be found under either of the following references :—

		PAGE
Barnum, H. L. Spy Unmasked, ...		924
Spy Unmasked, ...		924
Crosby, E., Memoirs of, ...		924
Birch, H., Memoirs of, ...		924

Again, take the following title :—

"2,112, D. A History of Three of the Judges of King Charles the First, Major General Whalley, General Goffe, and Colonel Dixwell, who, at the restoration in 1660, fled to America, and were concealed in Massachusetts and Connecticut for near thirty years; with an account of Mr. Theophilus Whale, supposed also to have been one of the Judges. By President Stiles. Hartford, 1794."

Here, besides the proper names Stiles, Whalley, Goffe, Dixwell, and Whale, I would index the word *Regicides*, under which, though it does not occur on the title-page, the book is likely to be looked for.

In a word, my system amounts to a copious multiplication of cross references.

For using the Index, therefore, the following simple rule will be prefixed to it. "If the author's, translator's, or annotator's name is known, turn to it. If the title only of a book is known, and not the author's name, or if it is anonymous, turn to the most important word, preferring of two words equally important that which stands first in the title. Otherwise, turn to the subject.

"Having found a book in this Index, the number in the outer column indicates that page in the Catalogue, to which turn in order to find the full title of the work, together with its number and size, which latter indicates to the Librarian its position on the shelves."

I flatter myself, that where this plan is carried out, the Library Company of Philadelphia will possess a Catalogue unsurpassed for facility of reference by any in the world.

The labor of Indexing the larger Catalogue of 1835 is nearly completed. It remains to consolidate the titles of books added since 1835 into a third volume, classified on the same plan as vols. 1 and 2, to index this third vol., and finally to arrange the whole Index matter alphabetically to form an Appendix. Volume 3, therefore, and Index, will probably be published about January, 1855.

INTERNATIONAL EXCHANGES.

The following communication, from Mons. Vattemare, was laid before the Convention by Mr. C. B. Norton:

PARIS, August 22, 1853.

DEAR SIR:—I take this opportunity to send you the accompanying series of tables, submitted some months ago to the Emperor, and prepared by order of his majesty.

The whole of my system is there; its origin and progress, and the results already obtained up to the year 1853.

But since these tables were presented to the Emperor, the Exchanges have considerably increased. Yet the above statement will give you an idea of what the result will be, the moment the system shall have been universally adopted and established upon a large and permanent basis; above all, when you consider what has been accomplished by so humble an individual as myself.

What I aim at is, the establishment of a regular and permanent system of exchange between governments, of not only the useless duplicates of their public libraries, but everything emanating from the genius of a nation, so as to form, in the Capitols of the civilized nations, public international libraries that would become a permanent exhibition of the intellectual power of each of them, a lasting World's Fair of the genius of nations. Hence, my constant and humble request has always been, while addressing myself to the government of your noble country, "whenever you shall be in want of a European book, buy an American book;" in Europe I make the same invitation. Let us have a central agency on each Continent, which shall be in connection with each other to negotiate these exchanges; let us have a monthly publication in English, French, and German, which shall publish the proceedings of the agency, and the titles of the books or objects exchanged, or to be exchanged. Would not such a plan powerfully contribute to the diffusion of knowledge and international goodwill, and to the realization of the republic of letters, the peaceful confederation of republics, kingdoms and empires? Could a greater assistance be given to the Book Trade than the adoption of such a plan?

The political events that have transpired since 1847, have brought a temporary prejudice to my system. On my return from America, I found the administration almost entirely renewed. I have had to do with officers entirely unacquainted with my mission, and uninterrupted changes and alterations in the different ministerial departments have rendered my task very difficult and extremely laborious. This is one of the only causes why the results have not been exactly what they promised to be when I left France for my mission to the United States; but a little patience, and things will take their proper course. The moment there shall be the slightest relaxation in the political excitement, attention will be immediately turned towards our system.

You know what Prince Napoleon said in your presence: that twice already he had had about our system a conversation with the Emperor, who told him that he appreciated the system most highly, and was only waiting for a moment of leisure to examine it thoroughly, and devise the means of realizing it.

Meanwhile, the Minister of Public Instruction, on the proposal of his colleague, the Minister of Public Works, has addressed a circular letter to the other members of the Cabinet, inviting them to form a kind of association to give to the system all the support it deserves. But before giving an official answer to this proposal, a general investigation is now taking place in all the departments, the public libraries, museums, &c., to ascertain what has already been received, and the results to be anticipated from the system.

The Minister of Public Instruction told me, some time ago, that this system would be of no value to the world, unless it be established upon a large scale; that, heretofore, all I had done, although very considerable, was a mere gleaning.

As for our American collection, you know, likewise, the opinion of Prince Napoleon, who considers it as "a great monument to the genius of a great people, and of its friendly feeling towards France." He thinks, also, that the place now ready to receive it, in the building of the Chamber of Commerce, is not becoming its importance, and he told me, in your presence, that he would himself see the new Prefect, to manage that matter with him to the honor of America and the gratification of the public. The projected arrangement is to give to each State a certain number of alcoves or shelves, in accordance with its intellectual riches and liberality, each one severally distinguished with its coat of arms and date of incorporation.

As for the system, it is gaining ground rapidly in Europe. By a letter dated St. Petersburg, 29th July last, received the same day I had the pleasure of seeing you, His Excellency the Baron de Korff, Counsellor of State, and Director of the Imperial Library of St. Petersburg, acknowledging the receipt of the Natural History of the State of New York, informs me that, after mature consideration, convinced of the important services our system of exchange is likely to render, he sends me the list of a series of most valuable duplicates of *incunabula* in the Imperial Library, to be placed at my disposal. The Danish Government has also presented, through its minister here, a list of splendid ancient works. The librarians of some of the celebrated Universities of Germany have made similar communications. I am waiting with the greatest anxiety for the official answer of the French administration, to be able to begin the publication of our Bulletin of international exchanges, to publish all those lists of most valuable works.

You have seen the fine series of ancient and modern books they were selecting for me at the Imperial Library. The little time you spent in my office was yet sufficient to give you an idea of what may be obtained from our system. You saw all the nations side by side, republicans and imperialists holding each other by the hand to help the realization of our great and peaceful Republic of Letters.

Let me close this letter by expressing my grateful acknowledgment towards the States and institutions of the Union, that have so readily and so nobly given a helping hand to my efforts, and tell them that, in my conviction, the time is not distant when they will reap the advantages of that generous and persevering support; that the little that has been done to this time is only the earnest of what is yet to come. As for the private individuals who have seconded my labors, the number is too great to mention them here, and they have already found in their conscience and patriotism the reward of their acts.

Yet allow me to mention one of them. I consider it to be my duty to name particularly, in order to express to him my sincerest gratitude for his constant and unrelaxed attention to our interests. I refer to Mr. E. Irving, of the Sample Office, New York. This gentleman, since my departure from America to the present time, has generously devoted his time, energies, and labors as agent, to receive and transmit the objects exchanged between our two Continents, without receiving the slightest compensation.

I would feel most happy, dear sir, if the Convention of American Librarians should consider the tables here annexed worthy of their attention, and I will be very thankful to you, if you will be kind enough to communicate to me their opinion. Have the kindness to say to these learned gentlemen, how happy I would have been to have found myself among so many distinguished savants, many of whom have shown themselves so benevolent to me, and in a country whose generous and fraternal hospitality I shall never forget.

Remain assured, dear sir, of the sentiments of esteem and friendship of your devoted friend,   ALEXANDRE VATTEMARE.

MR. C. B. NORTON.

List of Establishments which have Participated in the Benefits of the System of Exchanges.

Grand Duchy of Baden.
University of Heidelberg.

Belgium.
All the Ministerial Departments.
King's Library.
Royal   "
Royal Academy of Science.
City of Brussels.
"   Antwerp.
"   Liege.
Geographical establishment of Brussels.

The Netherlands.
All the Ministerial Departments.
King's Library.
Royal   "
Library of the General States.
University of Leyden.
Chamber of Commerce of Rotterdam.
Chamber of Commerce of Amsterdam.

France.
All the Ministerial Departments.
Chamber of Peers (Senate).
"   of Deputies (Legislative Body).
Post-office.
Court of Cassation.
"   Accounts.
Imperial Academy of Science.
"   "   Moral and Political Sciences.
Imperial Academy of Medicine.
Imperial Museum of Natural Hist.
School of Mines.
"   of Ponts et Chausses.
Normal School.
Geographical Society.
Asiatic Society.
Agricultural Society.
Horticultural   "
Geological   "

Society of Encouragement.
Imperial Library.
Library of the Louvre.
"   "   Sarbonne.
Private Library of the Emperor.
Imperial Printing House.
City of Paris.
"   Bordeaux.
"   Marseilles.
"   Metz.
"   Nantes.
"   Havre.
"   Rouen.

Russia.
Imperial Academy.
"   Library.
"   Botanical Garden.

Wurtemberg.
University of Tubingen.

United States of America.
All the Departments of the Federal Government.
The Presidential Residence.
Library of Congress.
Patent Office.
Office of Topographical Engineers.
U. S. Military Academy, West Point.
U. S. Naval Academy, Annapolis.
National Observatory, Washington.
Supreme Court of the U. S.
National Institute.
Military Academy of S. Carolina.
Academy of Science and Art, Boston.
National Academy of Design of New York.
Institute of Albany (N. Y.)
American Institute of New York.
Mechanics'   "   "
University of Georgetown, (D. C.)
University of Hanover, (N. H.)
"   Harvard, (Mass.)
"   Maryland.
College of Brunswick, (Me.)
"   Waterville, (Me.)

College of Burlington, (Vt.)
" New Haven, (Ct.)
" Columbia, (N. Y.)
" Geneva, (N. Y.)
" Rutgers, (N. J.)
" Annapolis, (Md.)
" Charlotteville, (Va.)
" Chapel Hill, (N. C.)
" Ann Harbor, (Mich.)
Brown University, Providence,(R.I.)
Union College, (N. Y.)
Society of Natural History of Port-
land, (Me.)
Society of Natural History of Boston.
" " of St. Louis, (Miss.)
Mercantile Library of Boston.
" " of New York.
" " of Springfield.
Agricultural Society of Massachu-
setts.
Agricultural Society of Boston.
" " Wilmington,(Del.)
Apprentices' Library of South Caro-
lina.
Historical Society of Brunswick,
(Me.)
Historical Society of Boston.
" " Worcester, (Mass.)

Historical Society of Hartford, (Ct.)
" " New York.
" " Trenton, (N. J.)
" " Baltimore.
" " Richmond, (Va.)
" " Savannah, (Ga.)
" " Upper Alton, (Ill.)
" " St. Louis, (Miss.)
" " Louisville (Ky.)
City of Washington, (D. C.)
" Bangor, (Me.)
" Portland, "
" Boston.
" Lowell, (Mass.)
" New York.
" Albany, (N. Y.)
City of Philadelphia, (Pa.)
" Baltimore, (Md.)
" Trenton, (N. J.)
" Hartford, (Ct.)
" Burlington, (Vt.)
" Providence, (R. I.)
City of Richmond, (Va.)
" Raleigh, (N. C.)
" Charleston, (S. C.)
" New Orleans, (La.)
" Savannah, (Ga.)
" Indianapolis, (Ia.)

---

*Chronological Table of Official Acts, Documents, &c., by which several Govern-
ments have accepted the principle or regulated the application of the system
of Exchange, from 1832 to 1853.*

January 22, 1832. Letter from M. Lichsenthaler, Director of the Royal
Library of Munich.
December 6, 1833. Letter from Count Maurice Diedrichstein, Director
of the *Imperial Museum and Library of Vienna.*
January 27, 1834. Letter from Count Charles de Bruhl, superintend-
ent general of the *Museum at Berlin*, in the name
of the *King.*
January 27, 1834. Letter from M. Hahn, in the name of the *King of
Denmark.*
August 1, 1836. Letter from Mr. Alexander Mordwinoff, for General
Count de Benkendorff, in the name of the *Em-
peror of Russia,*

March	6, 1836.	My first petition is reported, approved and referred to the Minister of Public Instruction by the *Chamber of Deputies.*
March	26, 1836.	Same reception by the *Chamber of Peers*, who refer it to the Ministers of the Interior and Public Instruction.
December	5, 1837.	Letter from Mr. Glover, librarian to the *Queen of England*, in the name of her majesty.
May	5, 1838.	The *British Parliament* receives favorably my petition; the *British Museum* authorized to open intercourse of exchanges with foreign establishments.
February	2, 1839.	My second petition reported, approved and referred, by the two *French Chambers*, to the Minister of Public Instruction and the President of the Council of Ministers.
February	17, 1840.	Deliberation of the *Royal Patriotic Society of Havana* adopting the system of exchange.
March	26, 1840.	Vote of $3,000, for international exchanges, by the *Senate of Louisiana.*
May	7, 1840.	*Senate of New York* approves the system of exchange.
July	17, 1840.	Bill of *Congress*, authorizing the exchanges of 50 extra copies of every document printed by Congress, to be printed and bound for that purpose.
February	6, 1841.	Sanction of the *Governor General of Canada.*
March	14, 1841.	Bill of the Legislature of the State of *Maine*, 50 extra copies of documents are to be printed and bound for international exchanges.
April	9, 1842.	My third petition is reported, approved and referred, by the *Chamber of Deputies*, to the Ministers of Foreign Affairs, Interior and Public Instruction.
April	29, 1842.	Same reception by the *Chamber of Peers*, as above, and referred to the same ministers.
December	21, 1842.	Deliberation of the *Municipal Council of Paris.*
	1847.	Appropriation of 3,000 fr., for international exchanges, voted to the *Department of Public Instruction.*
	1847.	Appropriation of a similar sum to the committee on the library of the *Chamber of Deputies.*
June	26, 1848.	Bill of *Congress.*
June	30, 1848.	Another bill of *Congress* of the United States, sanctioning the bill of 1840, and granting an appropriation to help on the system.
July	25, 1848.	Resolutions of the *Committee on the Library of Congress*, in relation to the same.
April	1850.	Presentation of several objects of exchanges to the *Chambers of Chili*, through A. Vattemare's agency.

174

April	1852.	Decision from the *Minister of the Interior of the Netherlands,* appointing A. Vattemare agent of the kingdom.
May	1852.	Decision of the *Minister of Finance of Belgium.*
July	29, 1853.	Letter from his Excellency, Baron de Korff, member of the Imperial Privy Council, Director of the Public Library of St. Petersburg.
July	15, 1853.	Letter and programme from the central committee for international exchange, appointed by the Minister of the Interior.

Seventeen States of the Union have adopted similar Laws to that of Congress, viz. :

Maine,	March,	1841–44–48.	Pennsylvania,	August,	1848.
Maryland,	"	1842.	Virginia,	September,1848.	
Indiana,	January,	1844–48.	S. Carolina,	December, 1848.	
Michigan,	March,	1844–48.	N. Hampshire,	January,	1849.
Massachusetts,	February,1845–49–50.		N. Carolina,	"	1849.
Rhode Island,	January,	1846.	Delaware,	March,	1849.
New York,	October,	1847.	Connecticut,	May,	1849.
Vermont,	Nov.,	1847.	Florida,	October,	1850,
New Jersey,	January,	1848.		and January,	1853.

Table of the Operation of the System of Exchanges, from 1847 to 1851, inclusive.

RECEIVED BY	BOOKS AND PAMPHLETS.	MAPS AND PLANS.	ENGRAVINGS.	MEDALS & COINS.
The United States of America,	30,655	1,607	807	1,288
France, ...	25,092	1,318	220	565
Foreign Governments, . .	5,264	711		30
Total amounts, . . .	61,011	3,636	1,027	1,883

To the above must be added, as received and distributed :

From France, the collection of weights and measures of France, 173 prepared birds, several cases of minerals, fossils and seeds.

From the United States, the collection of weights and measures of the U. S. ; six models of vessels and three of dry docks ; samples of the manufactures of Lowell, living animals, prepared birds, minerals, specimens of woods, seeds, the plaster cast of the head of a mastodon, fossils, a large specimen of oxydulated iron from the iron mountains of Missouri.

The following resolutions were presented by Mr. GUILD, and unanimously adopted :—

Resolved, That this Convention be regarded as preliminary to the formation of a permanent Librarians' Association.

Resolved, That a Committee of five be appointed to draft a Constitution and By-Laws for such an Association, and present them at the next meeting of the Convention.

Resolved, That when this Convention adjourn, it adjourn to meet in Washington City at such a time as the said Committee of five may appoint.

Resolved, That this Committee be requested, with reference to this adjourned meeting, to suggest topics for written communications or free discussion, and also to make such other arrangements as shall, in their judgment, be best adapted to meet the wants of the public, in regard to the whole subject of Libraries and library economy.

In accordance with these resolutions, the following gentlemen were appointed on the Committee for Permanent Organization :—Prof. C. C. Jewett, of Washington; Mr. Chas. Folsom, of Boston; S. Hastings Grant, of New York; Elijah Hayward, of Ohio, and R. A. Guild, of Providence

At the close of these deliberations the Convention adjourned, to meet in Washington, upon the call of the above Committee.

Notes

CHAPTER ONE

1. For list of delegates and their identification, see "Appendix" (p. 118 ff.).

2. See Abraham Flexner's *Daniel Coit Gilman, Creator of the American Type of University* (New York, 1946).

3. *Library Journal,* vol. 12, p. 510. November, 1887.

4. American Library Association. *Papers and Proceedings . . . 1886,* p. 1.

5. Willard L. Felt, president of the New York Mercantile Library, had this to say of Grant in his Annual Report for 1853 (January, 1854), p. 19: "To the Librarian, Mr. S. H. Grant, the Association are under many and great obligations. Eminently qualified by natural endowments for the situation which he has so long and so faithfully occupied, he has devoted himself to the discharge of its duties with the most commendable zeal and assiduity. The office is one of great labor and responsibility, and we have reason to congratulate ourselves that it is filled by one so well fitted for the position by his literary attainments and gentlemanly bearing."

6. *New York City During the American Revolution* (Privately printed for the [Mercantile Library] Association, 1861). S. H. Grant's name appears as a member of the Committee on the Tomlinson Collection only, not as compiler of the book. Arthur Hastings Grant, his son, in *The Grant Family* (1898), p. 227, was responsible for the statement that S. H.

Grant compiled the volume. Since *The Grant Family* was written during S. H. Grant's lifetime, and since, in 1861, he was librarian of the Mercantile Library it is undoubtedly true.

7. Vol. 2, p. 128.
8. Vol. 2, p. 168.
9. Vol. 3, p. 18.
10. Vol. 3, p. 38.
11. Vol. 3, p. 62.
12. Vol. 3, p. 82.
13. Anson Judd Upson, 1823-1902. See "Appendix," p. 125.
14. John Berrien Lindsley, 1822-1897. Physician, clergyman and educator; organized the Medical Department of the University of Nashville and became Chancellor in 1855. *(Dictionary of American Biography.)*
15. Charles Edwin West, 1809-1900. Principal of the Buffalo Female Academy, 1852-1860; later of Brooklyn, N. Y.; introduced the first college course for women. *(National Cyclopedia of American Biography,* vol. 8, p. 235.)

CHAPTER TWO

16. Vol. 3, p. 82.
17. The roster of delegates shows that T. W. Harris, Barnas Sears, E. C. Herrick, Joshua Leavitt, J. W. Chambers, Wm. E. Jillson, N. B. Shurtleff, L. M. Boltwood and George E. Day did not attend the Conference. For the other signers see "Appendix."
18. *Norton's Literary and Educational Register, for 1854,* p. 54-55.
19. Thaddeus William Harris, 1795-1856. Notable entomologist. *(Dictionary of American Biography.)*
20. Edward Claudius Herrick, 1811-1862. *(Ibid.)*
21. George Henry Moore, 1823-1892. *(Ibid.)*
22. William Alfred Jones, 1817-1900. *(Ibid.)*

23. Barnas Sears, 1802-1880. *(Ibid.)*
24. Lloyd Pearsall Smith, 1822-1886. *(Ibid.)*
25. William Frederick Poole, 1821-1894. *(Ibid.)*
26. The *Atlantic Monthly,* vol. 12, p. 665-679. December, 1863.
27. Edward Everett Hale, 1822-1909. *(Dictionary of American Biography.)*
28. Henry Barnard, 1811-1900. *(Ibid.)*
29. Nathaniel Bradstreet Shurtleff, 1810-1874. *(Ibid.)*
30. Joshua Leavitt, 1794-1873. *(Ibid.)*
31. Of the others who signed but did not attend the Conference, Lucius Manlius Boltwood (1825-1905) was librarian of Amherst College from 1852 to 1860, and achieved prominence as a historian and genealogist (memoir in *New England Historical and Genealogical Register,* vol. 59, p. 41-52); and George Edward Day (1815-1905), professor of Biblical Literature at Lane Theological Seminary, became Dean of the Divinity School at Yale. *(National Cyclopedia of American Biography,* vol. 13, p. 574.) John W. Chambers, then secretary of the Committee on Admissions, became secretary of the Trustees of the American Institute in 1858, and was librarian in 1860.
32. See "Appendix," p. 119-128 *passim.*
33. *(Ibid.)* p. 128.
34. Joseph Green Cogswell, 1786-1871. See "A Forgotten Trail Blazer" by Harry M. Lydenberg in *Essays Offered to Herbert Putnam,* ed. by Wm. W. Bishop and Andrew Keogh (1929), p. 302-314; also A. E. Ticknor's *Life of Joseph Green Cogswell* (1874).
35. Quoted in *Norton's Literary Gazette,* vol. 3, p. 82. May 15, 1853.
36. *Journal of Sacred Literature,* ed. by John Kitto, n.s., vol. 4, p. 227-228. April, 1853.
37. Thomas Watts, 1811-1869, was Panizzi's assistant, and later (1866-1869) Keeper of Printed Books at the British Museum.

He was distinguished for his remarkable ability as a selector of books in the lesser known European languages. He published a *Sketch of the History of the Welsh Language and Literature* (1869).

38. Grant papers. (American Library Association archives.)
39. Louis Alexander Fagan's *Life of Sir Anthony Panizzi* (1880), vol. 1, p. 170-171.
40. James Yates, librarian of the Public Library of Leeds, Yorkshire, attended also the first meeting of the Library Association in London the next year.
41. Messrs. Guild, Poole, and L. P. Smith, of the 1853 Conference, were among the sixteen Americans who attended the first conference of the Library Association in London in 1877.
42. Grant papers.
43. *(Ibid.)*
44. *(Ibid.)*
45. See p. 69 ff. and Note 83.
46. Grant papers.
47. *Norton's Literary Gazette,* vol. 3, p. 98. June 15, 1853.
48. James Lennox, 1800-1880. *(Dictionary of American Biography.)*
49. George Livermore, 1809-1865.
50. Edward Elbridge Salisbury, 1814-1901.
51. Peter Force, 1790-1868. *(Dictionary of American Biography.)*
52. John Carter Brown, 1797-1874. *(Ibid.)*
53. *Norton's Literary Gazette,* vol. 3, p. 130. August 15, 1853.
54. Grant papers.

CHAPTER THREE

55. Vol. 3, p. 170-176. October 15, 1853.
56. P. 49-94.
57. *(Ibid.),* p. 54-58.
58. *Library Journal,* vol. 12, p. 508. November, 1887.
59. See p. 119-128.

60. Theodoric Romeyn Beck, 1791-1855, also professor of Materia Medica, Albany Medical School, and editor of *The American Journal of Insanity*. *(Dictionary of American Biography.)*
61. Benjamin Pierce Johnson, 1793-1869. *(Ibid.)*
62. Adolph Frost, an Episcopal clergyman connected with St. Mary's Church, Burlington, N. J., and Burlington College. He died in Heibrunn, Germany, in 1865.
63. William MacDermott, 1825-   , a banker, for many years Secretary of the Norristown Library. (T. W. Bean's *History of Montgomery County, Pennsylvania* [1884], p. 481-483.)
64. Grant papers.
65. The Astor Library was opened to the public January 4, 1854.
66. Thomas Jefferson Bryan, 1800?-1870, presented this collection to the New York Historical Society in 1867. A catalogue, by Richard Grant White, was published in 1853.
67. Abbott's collection was on exhibit at the Stuyvesant Institute.
68. John Banvard, 1815-1891, was a painter, traveler and writer, who had published his *Pilgrimage to the Holy Land* just the year before. *(Dictionary of American Biography.)*
69. *Providence Journal,* September 20, 1853.
70. The Rev. Samuel Osgood, 1812-1880. See "Appendix," p. 123.
71. *Norton's Literary Gazette,* vol. 3, p. 170-171. October 15, 1853.
72. Charles Coffin Jewett's "Notices of Public Libraries in the United States of America" (Appendix to U. S. Smithsonian Institution. *Annual Report.* 4th. 1850.)

CHAPTER FOUR

73. In the *Gazette* the order of names is Jewett, Osgood and Guild, and the committee was requested to report its action at "the next annual meeting." In the more carefully edited *Register,* the order is Osgood, Jewett and Guild, and the word "annual" is omitted, the secretary, on second thought, perhaps being unwilling to commit the as yet unorganized body to an *annual* meeting.

74. Vol. 1, p. 90.
75. Vol. 2, p. 4.
76. Vol. 1, p. 55-56.
77. Evidently the publication which Smith had in mind was Henry Rowe Schoolcraft's monumental work, *Historical and Statistical Information Respecting the History, Conditions, and Prospects of the Indian Tribes of the United States.* 6 vols. (1851-1855), which was subsidized by the U.S. Government.
78. Vol. 3, p. 215. December 15, 1853.
79. Henry Coppée, 1821-1895. See "Appendix," p. 125.
80. A comedy by Jean Baptist Poquelin. Cf. Sir Walter Scott's *Heart of Midlothian,* the last paragraph.

CHAPTER FIVE

81. P. 54-58.
82. Elijah Hayward, 1786-1864. See "Appendix," p. 127.
83. "A Plan for Stereotyping Catalogues by Separate Titles; and Forming a General Stereotyped Catalogue of Public Libraries in the United States." (In the Association's *Proceedings, Fourth Meeting . . . August 1850* [Washington, 1851] p. 165-176.) The Smithsonian Publication No. 47 (1852), entitled *On the Construction of Catalogues of Libraries . . . and Their Publication by Means of Separate, Stereotyped Titles,* was a revision and amplification of his earlier paper. The 2nd edition of the Smithsonian issue was published in 1853, apparently just in time for the Conference (see p. 30-31).
84. Josiah Warren, 1798-1874, printer, inventor, reformer and anarchist. (*Dictionary of American Biography.*)
85. American Library Association. *Papers and Proceedings . . . 1886,* p. 1.
86. According to the *Catalogue Général* of the Bibliothèque Nationale the Cheveliar de Lagarde de La Pailleterie published *Lettre au directeur du "Moniteur Universel" réclam-*

ant la priorité de l'invention d'un procédé pour stéréotyper les catalogues des grandes bibliothèques, datée du 29 Septembre 1851. (Paris, n.d.) 4 p. 8 vo. The Bibliothèque Nationale lists no copy of the 1845 publication referred to, but does record an 1855 publication on the same subject.

87. Frederic Vinton, 1817-1890. See "Appendix," p. 127.

88. The others were Henry Barnard, Reuben A. Guild, Wm. F. Poole, Lloyd P. Smith, and John Wm. Wallace. Chas. Edw. West, who signed the call but did not attend the 1853 meeting, was present in 1876 at the inauguration of the American Library Association.

89. Halsey William Wilson, 1868-   , president of the H. W. Wilson Co., began the publication of the *Cumulative Book Index* in 1898.

90. Dr. Jewett would have been keenly interested in the great Union Catalogue at the Library of Congress, as well as the printed catalogue cards.

CHAPTER SIX

91. Dr. Guild was mistaken in referring to "the late" William Libri. This was the notorious Comte Guilliaume Libri (died in 1869) whose "noted" library of priceless manuscripts was made up largely of thefts from the libraries of France. (See Herbert Putnam's "The Romance of a Famous Library" in the *Atlantic Monthly*, vol. 81, p. 538-545. April, 1898.) The letter from which Dr. Guild quoted is to be found in the 1849 report of the Select Committee on Public Libraries. (Gt. Brit. *Parliamentary Papers*. 1849. [548] XVII, ¶1948, p. 118*-123*). It was entitled "Letter from M. Libri to W. Ewart, Esq., M.P., on the subject of the public libraries of France and Italy, 19 May 1849." The quotation used by Dr. Guild is found on p. 123*. Libri's letter is found in the proceedings of the Convention as given in the *Gazette* only. For some unknown reason it was omitted from the fuller

account in the *Register*—perhaps its author's reputation had been discovered.

92. Alexandre Vattemare, 1796-1864. (Sketch in New England Historic Genealogical Society. *Memorial Biographies.* vol. 5, p. 391-395. 1894.)

93. Georg Heinrich Pertz, 1795-1876, was the editor of the *Monumenta Germaniae historica,* then in course of publication, and secretary of the Royal Archives of Hanover.

94. Romain Merlin, 1793-1876, whose *Reflexions sur la catalogue des livres imprimés de la Bibliothèque Royale* (32 p.) was published in Paris in 1847.

95. *Norton's Literary and Educational Register, for 1854.* Merlin's letter on classification occupies p. 81-84; Vattemare's communication on international exchanges, p. 87-93.

96. Vol. 4, p. 286.

97. "The Character and Services of Alexandre Vattemare" by Josiah P. Quincy (in Massachusetts Historical Society. *Proceedings.* 1885. 2nd ser., vol. 1, p. 261.)

98. P. 87-91.

99. (*Ibid.*), p. 84-87.

100. *Norton's Literary Gazette,* vol. 3, p. 174. October 15, 1853.

101. This compliment to Mr. Folsom was reported in the *New York Herald,* September 18, 1853, p. 6.

CHAPTER SEVEN

102. Mr. R. W. G. Vail, Director of the New York Historical Society, in response to my request for information about Williams' proposal, wrote (April 3, 1946): "In going through the minutes of the Executive Committee and the general minutes of the Society, we found references to Mr. Williams' proposed index and the appointment of a committee to handle the matter, in December, 1851 (Executive Committee minutes). In the general minutes for January and February, 1852, there were reports of progress, and in these minutes

for January 4, 1853, a resolution was adopted approving the idea and voting to form an Index Association made up of those who would subscribe to the expense of the project. . . . So far as our records seem to show, the undertaking was never carried out."

103. Gorham Dummer Abbott, 1807-1874, clergyman and educator. The Spingler Institute was a girls' school. *(Dictionary of American Biography.)*

104. Julia Dean, 1836-1868, "one of the most beloved actresses of the theatrical annals of the country" was then in the heyday of her success. *(Ibid.)*

105. The *Gazette* account reads "Hale" but copy in the American Library Association archives is corrected to "Haven" in the handwriting of S. Hastings Grant. The *Register* account reads "Haven."

CHAPTER EIGHT

106. Grant papers.

107. American Library Association. *Papers and Proceedings . . . 1902,* p. 120-121.

108. Ezekiel A. Harris died about 1923-24. (Cf. *A.L.A. Handbook,* 1924.)

109. Those who attended the 1887 Conference were: Reuben A. Guild, who read a "Memorial Sketch of Prof. Charles C. Jewett" *(Library Journal,* vol. 12, p. 507-511), Chas. W. Jencks, Gen. Norton himself, and Wm. F. Poole, who was President of the American Library Association that year. Geo. M. Abbott, of Philadelphia, read his paper, "Some Recollections of Lloyd P. Smith" *(Ibid.,* p. 545-546), who died in 1886.

110. *Library Journal,* vol. 12, p. 526. November, 1887.

111. *(Ibid.)*

112. Vol. 3, p. 176. October 15, 1853.

Index

Abbott, Gorham Dummer, 92, 94, 123, 185
Abbott, Henry, 47
Akerman, Charles, 120
American Antiquarian Society, 91, 119
American Association for the Advancement of Science, 10, 11-12
American Geographical and Statistical Society, 21, 122
American Institute, N. Y., 122, 123
American Library Association, 3, 13-14, 20, 26, 70, 73, 94, 100, 103-105, 106, 116, 183, 185
Astor Library, 23, 46, 86, 124, 181

Bailey, Henry Mercer, 17, 120
Ballou, Sullivan, 120
Baltimore. Mercantile Library Association, 127
Banvard, John, 47, 124
Barnard, Henry 17, 21, 36, 103, 120, 183
Beck, Theodoric Romeyn, 45, 181
Boltwood, Lucius Manlius, 17, 178, 179
Boston Athenaeum, 12, 62, 119
Boston Mercantile Library Association, 61, 119
Boston Public Library, 104
Bourne, William Oland, 122
Bowdoin College, 119
Brooklyn Athenaeum, 125
Brown, John Carter, 37, 180

Brown University, 119
Bryan, Thomas Jefferson, 181
Buffalo Young Men's Asscociation, 125

Carrington Library, 120
Catalogs, Card, 83-84
Chambers, John W., 17, 179
Chapin, Edwin Hubbell, 17, 124
Cincinnati Mercantile Library Association, 127
Classification, Bibliographical, 75-78
Cogswell, Joseph Green, 23, 26, 31, 36, 46, 69, 179
College of New Jersey, 126
College of Physicians and Surgeons, 123
Columbia College, 121
Cooper, William, 126
Cooper Union, 122
Coppée, Henry, 62-64, 107-108, 125
Crosby, Howard, 64, 122
Curtis, W. P., 17, 22, 127

Day, George Edward, 17, 178, 179
Dean, Julia, 93, 185
Deeth, Sylvanus G., 126
DeWitt, Thomas, 122
Dickinson, James Taylor, 121
Disturnell, John, 97-98, 122
Dodge, Ossian Euclid, 118
Dodge, Robert, 118, 124
Dunbar, Edward Ely, 23, 128

186